ENRICO CARUSO

HIS RECORDED LEGACY

An unusual portrait of Enrico Caruso

Enrico Caruso

*His Recorded
Legacy*

by

J. FREESTONE

AND H. J. DRUMMOND

SIDGWICK AND JACKSON
LONDON

First published in 1960

© *J. Freestone and H. J. Drummond*

Printed in Great Britain by
Clarke, Doble and Brendon Ltd., Oakfield Press
Plymouth

PREFACE

THE aim of the authors of this little book is to give a complete list, chronologically arranged, of all Caruso's known recordings, together with notes on each record. Although a detailed and excellent series of articles by Mr. R. W. F. Potter was published in "The Gramophone" just over twenty-five years ago, this is, we believe, the first time that a complete critical analysis has been undertaken. This is no small task, but is made easier by the fact that Caruso's recording activities were not, as was the case with some other great singers, complicated by his transferring his services backwards and forwards from one company to another.

His first records were made for Pathé Frères by the Anglo Italian Commerce Co. probably in 1900. These were followed by the seven Zonophone records made for the Anglo Italian Commerce Co. early in 1902, and at almost the same time by his first G & T records, the last of which was made in the spring of 1904. A few weeks before this, Caruso made his first Victor records in New York, and after 1904 this company, (then affiliated to H.M.V.) was entrusted with making all recordings of his voice till his death. This has very much simplified the task of tracing all his records and arranging them in chronological order, a matter of great importance, since it enables a keen listener to follow the gradual maturing of Caruso's interpretative ability, and the changes which took place in his voice with the passing of the years.

Some artistes show little development and little change throughout the major part of their professional careers, but Caruso's voice became gradually darker and more voluminous as time passed by and at the time of his death some of the easy unforced head resonance of his prime had gone, and was replaced by a compelling majesty of delivery not unmixed with a tendency to hardness.

In his prime, Caruso's voice was of a beauty impossible to describe in mere words. It was a lyric tenor of considerable power, a voice of gold with a velvety covering to the lower range, and an easy ring to the head notes which suggested an almost complete lack of muscular effort, and gave a liquid fluency to all his singing. With the passing of years the "velvet" began to wear thin in places, and the liquid quality gave place to a hardness which indicated the employment of greater effort. Until his death, however, Caruso's voice retained much of that original beauty which made it unique among tenors.

His technique was so perfect in his prime that he was able to concentrate all his intense musical feeling upon whatever he was singing, and he seldom if ever called attention to this technique at the expense of the musical whole. He was scrupulously accurate in his fidelity to the composer's intentions, apart from the customary and traditional cadenzas in the early Italian operas, and he had the ability to colour his voice to suit all operatic occasions. Added to this, his unerring musical instinct enabled him to light instantly upon the climax of each particular aria, and then he brought his unsurpassed technique to the task of building up each composition in such a way that all his work carried a burning conviction and a sense of inevitability so that we feel it is no longer a singer singing an aria, but a man expressing his every emotion in the medium which is most natural to him.

Many of the records discussed in the following pages are no longer generally available, but others are frequently met with on the shelves or in the lists of second hand record dealers. As is to be expected, where the records have long been obsolete and no shells exist, high prices are paid for any copies which change hands.

It is significant that many of Caruso's contemporaries are purely "Collectors' artistes" such as Anselmi, Bonci, De Lucia, while his records have a great appeal to the general public, and are often broadcast in response to wide demand, while many transcriptions have recently appeared on long playing records, with in some cases a later orchestral accompaniment superimposed on the old one, and in many other instances a false echo has been added in a mistaken attempt to give "life" to the original record. In the opinion of the authors such recordings, while of possibly greater appeal to the undiscriminating general public, will never replace the original recordings which give a much better impression of the great tenor's voice.

A minor but we think not unimportant feature of this book is that it gives for the first time, as far as we are aware, a correct record of the venues of Caruso's many recording sessions. This is perhaps not merely a matter of more general interest, but also something that throws light on the reproduction of Caruso's voice at the various sessions. For example it is often assumed that the difference in Caruso's voice as heard on the Milan recordings, and those made for the Victor Company, is wholly accounted for by the passage of the years, and by different processes of recording. Is it not however possible that the acoustic properties of the various venues of recording had something to do with this? In the note on "Mattinata" it is pointed out that the quality of the voice is more like that of the 1902 series than that of the Victors of 1904, and yet "Mattinata" was recorded later than the first batch of Victors. The 1904 Victors too—recorded in room 826 of the Carnegie Hall New York—are more forward and the voice is darker than those of the 1905 and 1906 sessions. Is it not likely that the studios in which the records were made had much to do with this?

In addition to the venues of recording, the dates are also given together with the catalogue numbers of the records in both single and double sided forms, as well as the matrix numbers.

The following abbreviations are used throughout the book : S/S Cat. No. for Single sided Catalogue Number, D/S Cat. No. for Double sided Catalogue Number.

The records have been arranged in strict chronological order except in one or two special cases, and the date of recording is given above the title. Where several discs were made on the same day, the date is not repeated before each title, but will be found above the first selection in that particular group. Exceptions to strict chronological listing will be found in the case of the concerted Faust excerpts, which have been grouped together for convenience, and in such cases the date is given separately with each recording.

The changes in recording methods are noted elsewhere in the book, as well as the appearance and general characteristics of the early issues. Details are also given concerning the existence or otherwise of the original shells, and it is hoped that the novice and general collector may be helped in his selection of items to obtain a representative collection of the great Italian's records. They cannot of course compare technically with modern recording, although the voice itself is generally faithfully presented, while the phrasing and the sincerity of the artist are for all to hear, and are indeed our common heritage.

vii

FOREWORD

Thirty-six years ago I wrote about Caruso: "He is really the Dickens of singing; he may overdo a sob occasionally, but we forgive him for his rich human sympathy and his abounding vitality. And all his last records! That marvellous *Largo* in which his voice peals like a mighty organ, and at the very end that *Addio a Napoli* sung so gaily without an inkling that it was indeed for ever 'addio'. Yes, it was, nay, it is a great voice. It holds within its variety the orange groves of Sorrento, the sparkling ripples of Santa Lucia, the raucous street-cries of Naples, and the calm blue expanse of the lovely bay. It is sometimes rugged as the trunk of the great ilex trees above Castellamare and sometimes soft (as in that marvellous last note of *Magiche note*) as the sea-wind in the boughs of an Aleppo pine. It is as profoundly coloured as the grottos of Capri, as passionate as the Italian sun, as velvety as the Italian sky, and sometimes as murky as the crater of Vesuvius. There are three things in this life that seem to store up the warmth of dead summers, pot-pourri and wine and the records of a great singer. As you read this, somewhere somebody in the world is playing a Caruso record, and somewhere somebody is getting from it an assurance that life is worth while. His immortality is secure, for every day somewhere somebody will hear his voice for the first time and say 'This was a singer'."

I repeat those words to-day, as much convinced of their truth as I was when I wrote them, and it gives me much pleasure to be able to repeat them in a foreword to the remarkable feat of industry, accuracy, and judgment performed by Canon Drummond and Mr. Freestone, to which I pay tribute.

I do not hesitate to suggest that his master's voice heard by that fox-terrier was the voice of Caruso himself, for none knows better than the Gramophone Company what the gramophone owes to Caruso.

It was the reproduction of that glorious voice which assured the world of what the gramophone would one day accomplish. No tenor

ix

that has risen to fame since Caruso with the help of electric recording could have done as much. It was his ability to inspire a horn with his own pulsating life which captivated us over fifty years ago.

Canon Drummond and Mr. Freestone have administered this great legacy of song without extravagance and I shall confidently claim that their book will remain permanently indispensable to the ever growing number of connoisseurs and collectors.

COMPTON MACKENZIE

To George T. Keating

ACKNOWLEDGMENTS

The authors wish to express their deep appreciation of the help and encouragement which they have received from their many friends in the collecting world, and in particular from the late Eric Bernard and the late H. Hugh Harvey, and the R.C.A. Victor Division of the Radio Corporation of America.

THE PATHÉ RECORDS

THE chief interest attaching to the three records known as "Pathé" records, lies in the fact that they are the first ones Caruso made. The exact date of their recording may now never be known, but we are able to bring it down within fairly narrow limits. Tosca only had its world première in January, 1900, and the records were on sale on the continent before the end of that year. They must therefore have been recorded in 1900, and not as some have thought, as late as 1901.

The original cylinders seem to have been those of $3\frac{1}{2}$ inches diameter, often spoken of as "middle size" or "Inter" to distinguish them from the subsequently issued cylinders which had diameters of just over two inches, and the "Stentor" and "Celeste" issues with their five inch diameters.

As is well known, these three numbers were afterwards transferred to vertically cut track discs, (both eleven and fourteen inches), playing from the centre outwards at a speed of about 120 revolutions a minute. Still later they were issued as 10 inch regular cut discs at speed 78.

While much about the early histories of these records is uncertain it is worth remembering that strictly speaking they are not Pathé recordings. Though made for and handled by Pathé Frères, they are all announced as being made by the Anglo Italian Commerce Co., and this incidentally is evidence that they were not made, as many have thought in France or Belgium, but in Italy, and in all probability in Milan.

It will not have escaped notice that none of Caruso's Pathé records occupies quite two minutes, even with the announcement. The choice of the Tosca and Huguenots arias was no doubt governed by the exigencies of the time available for cylinder recordings in those early days. The Huguenots number, and the Stornella were easily sung within the imposed limits, but Caruso has to hurry his singing of the Tosca aria in order to finish in time, and the piano is heard before the announcement is completed.

1

The following records were all made in Milan in 1900

TOSCA (Puccini) **"E lucevan le stelle".**

> Pathé disc, 84004, and later Emerson 301 vertically cut ("hill and dale")
> 6 inch disc, aria incompletely given. Herrold 500 (10 inch disc, regular cut).

The aria is sung with great ease of production, but it lacks the polish of the later versions. Caruso was apparently instructed to sing out, and not to employ mezza voce, and his voice sounds less covered, and less smooth than it subsequently did. How much this is due to the primitive recording, and how much to his comparative immaturity, it is now impossible to say. There is a warmth in his lower notes even at this early stage in his career, and the unmistakable timbre is already there in some measure, but the disc is not really of much musical interest, although, of course, historically it has great significance.

It is a matter of personal interest that this recording was in all probability made within a few weeks of Puccini taking from Caruso the opportunity of creating the role of Cavaradossi, which caused the tenor such bitter disappointment at the time.

GLI UGONOTTI (Meyerbeer) **"Qui sotto il ciel".**

> Anglo Italian Commerce Co. cylinder 84006. Pathé disc (11 or 14 inches)
> 84006, vertical cut. Collectors Record Shop No. 6 (10 inch regular cut).

This brief aria, is Raoul's first entrance, and Caruso again sings with freedom, and apparent abandon. The voice is clear and high, and there is a hint, but only a hint of the matchless quality of his unique organ.

"Tu non mi vuoi più bene". Stornello.

> Anglo Italian Commerce Co. Cylinder 84003. Pathé disc (11 or 14 inches)
> 84003, vertical cut. Collectors Record Shop No. 6, (10 inch regular cut).

This is a very ordinary Italian song sung without any real contrast, but with a clear bright voice. Caruso's feeling for words is already apparent, and his diction is excellent.

THE ZONOPHONE RECORDS

THE Seven Zonophone records which Caruso made for the Anglo Italian Commerce Company in Milan in the early part of 1902, are generally believed to be the first needle cut discs he ever made. For this reason and because of their great rarity as well as for their intrinsic artistic merits, they are most highly prized by collectors.

Long continued research has failed definitely to establish the exact date of these recordings. The very brief life of the Anglo Italian Commerce Company is responsible for both the extreme rarity of these records, and also to a great extent for the uncertainty which exists about their history. They were never on any English catalogue, and any copies of them which reached this country must have been imported from the Continent to special orders. They were however still listed on the Spanish Zonophone catalogue for February 1905, and on the French one for May of that year. Nevertheless they must have disappeared very soon after this, for they are all missing from the French catalogue for November 1906, and probably they vanished from other Continental catalogues at about the same time. At the period at which these records were made, the original shells would be backed up and used as stampers, and they were no doubt soon worn out, which would mean the end of these particular recordings. It is as certain as anything can be that all the shells of Caruso's Zonophones ceased to exist in about 1906, and as the records themselves had a selling history of only about four years, their great rarity is easily accounted for. They are indeed collectors' prizes and already command in America the highest prices of all Caruso's records, and there can be little doubt that their value will greatly increase.

Though the tradition in Italy is in favour of the Zonophone records having been made before those which the late Mr. F. W. Gaisberg made for the Gramophone and Typewriter Company—and this may well be true—we feel less sure of it than we did when the article on the seven Zonophone records which appeared in the September 1939 issue of "The Gramophone" was written.

Mr. Gaisberg himself once told the present writer that he thought we ought not to rule out the possibility of the Zonophone records having been made just after his own records, in emulation of their sensational success. And what weighs with us on the side of this conjecture more than it once did, is the difficulty we have in thinking that so busy a man as Caruso was in 1902 found time for the Zonophone recordings during the seven or ten days which were all that separated Germania's world première from the date of the Gramophone and Typewriter recordings. We had hoped at one time that the lettering on the Zonophone labels, where the singer is called "Signor Cav. Enrico Caruso" might throw some light on the date of the recording, but so far this hope has not been realized. All we can be sure of is that only a very few days separated these two recording sessions.

As many collectors will never have an opportunity of seeing one of these records, here is a brief description of their external characteristics. They have a slightly larger circumference than the Gramophone and Typewriter discs, their diameters being $10\frac{1}{8}$ inches, compared with the 10 inches of the G & T records, and they play for a little longer time. They have light blue labels which are quite flush with the records. In large gold letters just within the circumference are written the words, "Disco Zonofono" and under these, just above the centre hole are the words "International Zonophone Company". In the case of the two songs, their titles "Un bacio ancora" and "Luna fedel" are printed immediately below the centre hole, and then beneath the titles the names of the composers. Below these are the words "Tenore solo", then the singer's name, given on all these Zonophone labels as "Signor Cav. Enrico Caruso", then "Milano" and finally the catalogue number of the record. In the case of the five operatic numbers, the name of the aria is always printed in large letters immediately below the centre hole, and under this the name of the opera in much smaller type. The name of the composer is not given on the label of any of the operatic records.

While the labels are thus uniform in character, the backs of the earliest issues of these single sided discs are of two distinct types. One has the word "The Anglo Italian Commerce Co : Genova—Milano" within an outer circle, while within an inner circle are the words "Marcia depositata", and below them the large letters "A.I.C.C." and again below them "I migliori del mondo". An interesting feature of this type of back is that about half an inch from the centre hole is a circular indentation evidently intended to receive a pin attached to the turntable to prevent the record slipping. The second type of back is the one familiar to those who remember the English Zonophone record

4

in its single sided form, during the first few years of this century, with the word "Zonophone" twice stamped at right angles across the whole back of the record, and "Trade Mark" printed twice. On both types are found the words "Printed in Germany". It is perhaps not quite certain which of these two types is the older one, but it seems probable from their greater thickness and from the fact that they usually show most signs of wear, that the last described type is the original one. This was the opinion at Hayes though of course they have never handled these Zonophone records. In what are evidently later issues, the backs are sometimes quite plain and embossed numerals are found on the faces of the discs, instead of the earlier etched ones.

Passing from the external to the internal characteristics of these records, the one which would undoubtedly first strike a hearer would be that the volume of sound is lighter, and less forward than that heard on the G & T records. At the same time it should be said that Caruso's Zonophone records are very free from the blasting which was so common in those early days, when there was any overloading in volume, and also that it is not merely the great tenor's style and phrasing which are preserved to us on these seven discs; no one who was familiar with Caruso's voice can doubt on hearing them that he is listening to a real reproduction of it. We have spoken of Caruso's style and phrasing, and it is his renderings of some, at any rate, of these titles which make his Zonophone records so valuable. For, on the whole, they reveal Caruso in a different vein from that of the joyous irresponsibility which it has been said characterised most of the G & T recordings. It is a more restrained and perhaps we may say a more contemplative singer that we listen to on the Zonophones than on the familiar G & T's. "Un bacio ancora", "Luna fedel", "Una furtiva lagrima", the Germania aria, and the Siciliana from Cavalleria Rusticana are examples of what we mean. Four of these titles were recorded by Mr. F. W. Gaisberg and his brother Mr. W. C. Gaisberg in Milan, and it is interesting and instructive to contrast the renderings on the records made for the Anglo Italian Commerce Co., with those made for the Gramophone and Typewriter Co.

All Caruso's Zonophone records are "announced" records, the announcements being made as expeditiously as possible. The singer's name is not given—as it is on the three Pathé numbers—nor is the composer's except in the case of "Un bacio ancora", nor is any mention made—as it is on the Pathé numbers—of the company for which the record is being made. The two ballads are announced thus—"Un bacio ancora—Trimarchi" and "Luna fedel—Serenata". In the five operatic titles the name of the opera is first given followed by the title of the aria. An interesting point which arises from these announcements is whether or not Caruso is himself the announcer. On this the opinions of those qualified to give them, differ. Neither of the authors of this book knew Caruso personally, though one of them heard him sing several times, so they do not feel able to pronounce any opinion, but the well known collector Mr. Hugh Harvey who knew the great tenor personally, and was familiar with his speaking voice, strongly inclined to the opinion that Caruso himself makes the announcements on his Zonophone records.

All the Zonophone records were made in Milan in 1902.

"Un bacio ancora" (Trimarchi).

If Caruso's Zonophones are his rarest records, we think there is little doubt that "Un bacio ancora" and "Luna fedel", the two ballad recordings, are, as would be expected, the rarest of his Zonophone records. Very few copies indeed of these two numbers seem to have survived the vicissitudes of the years. Of the two we much prefer "Un bacio ancora" as a song, and it is the only number of this series which Caruso never recorded on any other occasion. Musically it is no more than "a song of its period" as the late Mr. F. W. Gaisberg once said to the present writer as they listened to this record together. From this one composition, one would imagine that Trimarchi was a kind of Italian Stephen Adams, but in spite of this "Un bacio ancora" is a record which affords a delightful specimen of Caruso's singing in those early days, for it suits him so well that it might have been written for him. It is beautifully sung—I recall Mr. Gaisberg's comment—"Caruso makes it"—in that mood of pensive sadness which Caruso interpreted so well, the mood in which we hear him in the 1908 "Ai nostri monti" duet with Louise Homer, in Massenet's "Elégie" or in "Si vous l'aviez compris".

"Luna fedel" (Denza) X. 1551.

This is surely one of the poorest songs ever recorded by Caruso, and it is not easy to think of the composer of "Occhi di fata", "Si vous l'aviez compris" and "Funicula, funicula", as the composer of it. We do, however, think the Zonophone version is in every way—except for the

6

much less forward recording—superior to the G & T one. Caruso takes about three quarters of a minute longer over this serenata on the Zonophone disc, and is evidently doing all he can to make the most of unattractive material. There is no false start in X. 1551 as there is in 52442.

L'ELISIR D'AMORE (Donizetti) **"Una furtiva lagrima"** X. 1552.

We think the tenor setting out to sing both stanzas of this aria on one side of a ten inch record must feel very much as would the French officer to whom Napoleon is supposed to have said "I can give you everything but time; remember the world only took six days to make". Caruso manages to get about half a minute longer on X. 1552 than on 52346 and this proves a real gain in his singing of the first stanza, but when he comes to "Un solo istante i palpiti" one feels that he is singing against time, as is alas the case with every Caruso version of this famous aria, except his first Victor recording of it when he devoted two discs to it in order that it should be sung in correct tempo.

TOSCA (Puccini) **"E lucevan le stelle"** X. 1553

This record of Puccini's well known aria does not call for much special comment, as it closely resembles the G & T one (D.A. 547) as a rendering, although it is musically accurate, and not like the March 1902 G & T version. Caruso of course, often re-recorded favourite titles, but only "E lucevan le stelle" and "Celeste Aida" were honoured by being recorded by him on five occasions—the two discs devoted to the recording of the "L'Elisir d'amore" aria in 1904 count, properly speaking as one recording. "E lucevan le stelle" is the only title which found a place in all Caruso's earliest recordings—Pathé, Zonophone, first G & T session and the first batch of Victors. All these have piano accompaniments but in November 1909 Caruso recorded it for the fifth and last time, and with orchestral accompaniment. This Zonophone recording of the aria is sung at a slower tempo than the Pathé rendering (1 minute 45 seconds) but at a faster one than the G & T and first Victor (2 minutes 4 seconds each), and is almost exactly the same in tempo as the final Victor (1 minute 56 seconds).

GERMANIA (Franchetti) **"No non chiuder gli occhi vaghi"** X. 1554.

Like its companion number on G & T, this is very beautifully sung, and perhaps there is greater warmth, and even more style in the ex-

7

quisite moulding of the phrases, but the melting mezza voce of the G & T version is not caught in this recording, and for that reason the G & T is much preferable, although both are splendid examples of Caruso's singing at its lyrical best.

RIGOLETTO (Verdi) "La donna è mobile" X. 1555.

This is an interesting record because it is the first Caruso rendering we have of this famous number, and we have to wait two years for the next one. The pianist thoroughly enjoys himself, and emphasises the rhythm of the music with amusing spirit. Caruso uses his voice with style and contrast and his mezza voce on "muta d'accento" is quite delightful. The ending is quite different from that of the Victor versions of 1904 and 1908.

CAVALLERIA RUSTICANA (Mascagni) "Siciliana" X. 1556.

This is we think, unquestionably the best of the Zonophone records. As a rendering it is perhaps not quite equal to the 1910 one—the late Herman Klein thought that the Siciliana on 7-52018 was Caruso's high water mark—but it is sung with wonderful ease and with greater artistic balance and emotional force than either of its two successors (52418 and 52064) which are neither of them among the best of their respective batches. (I cannot subscribe to this view, and my own mint original copy of 52418 is a great favourite of mine. There are traces of some discomfort in the high tessitura at the end, but the recording is so vivid, and the rendering so full of élan, that I am quite captivated by it. J.F.) Of course the earliest versions of Mascagni's aria do not equal the final one as a reproduction of Caruso's voice, but here again we think more than any of the other six Zonophones, it has recaptured the warmth and beauty of Caruso's marvellous organ. The absence of heavily covered tone in the final phrases is in noticeable contrast to his singing of them on 7-52018.

THE G & T RECORDS

Iᴛ is hardly possible to exaggerate the importance, in the history of recording, of the records made by Caruso for the Gramophone and Typewriter Company in 1902, at the Grand Hotel in Milan. In the late F. W. Gaisberg's reminiscences, "Music on Record", under Caruso's photograph are the words, "He made the Gramophone", and the fact that the great singer ultimately received over £1,000,000 in royalties on his H.M.V. and Victor records, is proof enough that these words were no mere figure of speech. Mr. Gaisberg, who recorded Caruso on that memorable occasion when he made his first G & T records has told us that directly he heard Caruso's voice, he knew it was "the voice the recording man had dreamed of". In those early days, the recorder of the human voice was between Scylla and Charibdis. If the singer was placed near the recording horn, his voice blasted, and if he was further away, his mezza voce singing was lost in the needle scratch. Caruso's voice, Mr. Gaisberg has told us, solved all these problems, and many others too, and as Sir Compton Mackenzie has said, at a time, "when violin solos sounded like bluebottles on a window pane, overtures like badly played mouth organs, chamber music like amorous cats, brass bands like run-away steam rollers, and pianos like an old woman clicking her false teeth, Caruso's voice proclaimed a millenium and preserved our faith".

At this first session, Mr. Gaisberg was assisted by his brother Mr. W. C. Gaisberg, and it is from the latter's very interesting recollections of it, as given in the first number of "The Voice" (January 1917) that we are able to fix the date as approximately March 18th, for he tells us there that it was about a week after the world première of Germania, which "went up" as opera people say, on March 11th. Mr. W. C. Gaisberg says in this article on Caruso, "I well remember him drawing a caricature of me as I stood at the recording machine", and in later years, Mr. F. W. Gaisberg described how the waxes were put on one after the other, without loss of time, Caruso being eager to get away for his lunch. Four of the shells of the records made at this March 1902 session, have long since perished, and copies of them in good condition are among collectors' most treasured prizes.

Mr. F. W. Gaisberg was not present at the second session held in November, 1902, when Mr. W. C. Gaisberg recorded another ten titles, and when the Grand Hotel Milan was once again the venue. The evidence for the November date seems conclusive. The Gramophone Company have in their registers, which they only received from Germany in about 1936, a note of the exact date of this recording—November 12th, 1902. Incidentally we know from Bruno Zirato's appendices to Pierre V. R. Key's "Enrico Caruso" that the tenor was in Milan at this date singing in Cilea's "Adriana Lecouvreur" in which he created the role of Count Maurizio on the evening of November 6th. Three of the records made at this session—the *"Adriana"* and *"Fedora"* arias and *"Luna Fedel"*—were not issued until later in 1903 than the other seven, and are often given as 1903 recordings but the evidence that they were made at the same time as the rest, is very strong. The attempt to detach them then from the November 1902 session is not supported at Hayes, and certainly finds no confirmation in their matrix numbers.

All the Milan records were naturally issued in this country soon after their recording, and their success was immense and instantaneous Mr. F. W. Gaisberg told the writer that the Company made £13,000 profit within six months on the ten records made at that first March session.

The following ten records were made in Milan in March, 1902

RIGOLETTO (Verdi) **"Questa o quella".**

Matrix No. 1783. First and only G & T Cat. No. 52344.

This record only had about six years of selling history, for it first failed to make its appearance in the July-August, 1908 H.M.V. Catalogue. It has never been in print in the United States. Of the twenty-two records altogether made by Caruso for the Gramophone and Typewriter Company, no less than fourteen found their way into the No. 2 catalogue, after being withdrawn from the H.M.V. General Catalogue, and there enjoyed a life only terminated by the outbreak of the second world war. Of the eight which failed to survive, five did so because their shells had perished. Of the remaining three, of which the shells still exist, and which were presumably not thought of sufficient interest to be given a place in the No. 2 list, "Questa o quella" is one.

This is a disappointing record, from a vocal point of view. The voice sounds constrained, and the top notes lack the usual ring so characteristic of Caruso. In addition the rhythm is less incisive than in the 1908 version. There is also little suggestion of the cynical character of the Duke. The ornaments are precisely the same as in the 1904 and 1908 recordings.

MANON (Massenet) "O dolce incanto".

Matrix No. 1785. First and only Cat. No. 52345.

This record has had an honoured history. It was retained on the H.M.V. general catalogue for about ten years, and when, some twelve years later, after its disappearance from the General Catalogue it was transferred to the No. 2 list in 1924, it still kept its single sided form, and original catalogue number until its deletion in 1946. It has now, in October 1951, made a welcome re-appearance in the H.M.V. Archive Series on V.A. 58. Until this issue, it had never been in print in the United States.

It is one of the best of the 1902 records, for all round merit. The voice is beautifully modulated, and the atmosphere well caught. Caruso does not sing the high "A" as written. The composer marks it as starting pianissimo, swelling out, and then returning to pianissimo. Caruso starts it softly, making a gradual crescendo, and finishing it forte— while De Lucia in his first recording does just the opposite! There are a few quite unnecessary intrusive "H's", but all in all, this is an excellent record.

L'ELISIR D'AMORE (Donizetti) "Una furtiva lagrima".

Matrix No. 1786. First and only Cat. No. 52346.

This record had a very short life, first failing to make its appearance in the H.M.V. September, 1907 Catalogue. The shell is one of the five of the Milan recordings which no longer exists. These facts mean that this is a rare record (though not so rare as the Zonophone record of the same title), and those who possess copies of it are fortunate. It has never been in print in the United States.

This is another good example of the first G & T recordings. The voice is well controlled and the rendering stylish and lyrical. The intrusive "H" is used a little excessively and there is an obvious example of "lipping" on the last word of the first verse—"vedo". (N.B. Lipping is the name given to the breaking of the voice at some point in a long

11

and gradual diminuendo. It is almost impossible to avoid it completely, and some of Bonci's records show the same fault. It would probably be quite unnoticeable on the stage).

The cadenza is sung with good agility, and the vocal tone throughout is well poised and of lovely quality.

MEFISTOFELE (Boito) "Giunto sul passo l'estremo".
Matrix No. 1787. S/S Cat. No. 52347. D/S Cat. No. D.A. 550.

This record, after remaining on the H.M.V. General Catalogue for about seven years, was transferred to the No. 2 list in 1924, under the catalogue number D.A. 550, being coupled with the November, 1902 "Dai Campi" (Matrix No. 2871). In this form it was not withdrawn till 1942. It had never been issued in U.S.A. till the Archive Series was brought out, but was then made available on V.A. 7, with the same coupling that it had in 1924.

Both this and the "Dai Campi" of the first series are most carefully sung. The tone in this record is well suited to the character of the aged Faust, who has at last found peace and contentment. This is undoubtedly one of the best records of this first series, and the voice is poised, even, and strikingly lyrical in character.

MEFISTOFELE (Boito) "Dai campi, dai prati".
Matrix No. 1789. Only Cat. No. 52348.

The shell of this record was "burnt up" to quote the late F. W. Gaisberg's words to the writer, before the end of 1902. Those were the days before the process of copying originals was discovered, when, as we have explained, shells had to be used as stampers. This record is therefore, in a special sense a collector's prize, since no more pressings from the original shell can ever be made, or have been made, since 1902. Perhaps on no records of which the shell does not exist, is such a fine reproduction of Caruso's voice to be heard. An interesting feature of this record is that it contains a false start by the singer. It has, of course, never been issued in America.

Apart from the barely noticeable false start, already mentioned, this is again most beautifully sung. Note the long, perfectly controlled diminuendo on "Di sacro mister". Caruso's mezza voce was never lovelier than in these early records. It has a unique fulness and a certain masculinity which distinguishes it from that of almost all other tenors.

12

TOSCA (Puccini) "E lucevan le stelle".

Matrix No. 1790. S/S Cat. No. 52349. D/S Cat. No. D.A. 547.

Caruso's third "E lucevan le stelle" is, as is the 1904 recording of this aria, sung at a slightly slower tempo than is any of the other renderings. After remaining on the General Catalogue for about seven years, (and probably being responsible for the exclusion of the 1904 recording from the English Catalogues until its appearance in October, 1951 in the first issue of the H.M.V. "Archive" Series as V.A. 34)., it reappeared in 1924, backed by the 1902 "Cielo e mar" and was transferred to the No. 2 Catalogue as D.A. 547, where it held its place till 1942. It has been re-issued in the Archive Series as V.A. 29, with the same backing as in 1924. It was issued in U.S.A. by the Victor Company (Catalogue numbers 5010 and 91,009) in October, 1903, when Caruso was first setting foot on United States soil (November 11th), but was withdrawn in the following year for their own recording of this title in February, 1904, and has now re-appeared there as V.A. 29.

Something very strange happens in this recording. Caruso starts the recitative three bars early, and sings the first phrase on "B" natural instead of "F" sharp. After this there is a gradual alignment of forces and some quick thinking on the part of the accompanist, and he and the singer are finally at one on the phrase "E un passo sfiorava la rena". Henceforward the record is a good one, but one can imagine the composer's reactions when he first heard it! No doubt the record would have been re-made if time had permitted. Certainly no such inaccuracies could possibly be passed today.

It is rather curious that so little has been written about this most obvious of all false starts in this first recording session for G & T.

IRIS (Mascagni) "Serenata".

Matrix No. 1791. Only Cat. No. 52368.

This is one of the five G & T's of which the shell has perished. As it had disappeared before the issue of the March, 1908 Catalogue, it is a record much prized for its rarity, and no doubt all the more so because Caruso did not record this title on any other occasion. This record seems to have been less successful than most in standing up to the steel needles which were the only kind available in those early days. As a consequence, copies of it in really good condition are not easy to find. It has never been issued in America.

Apart from its rarity, this record has considerable merit. The composer's markings are well followed, although the phrasing at the words "Ma ti faro morir dal sol baciata" is unusual. It is nevertheless highly effective, and the aria is sung lyrically and with great sincerity. The high notes are not entirely free from a sense of effort in one or two places.

AIDA (Verdi) "Celeste Aida".

Matrix No. 1784. Only Cat. No. 52369.

The first of Caruso's five renderings of this famous aria is another collector's treasure, for with the first "Dai Campi" its shell was "burnt up" before the end of 1902. It is therefore one of the twelve Caruso records of which no pressings have been made for over fifty years, and no more can ever be issued. It was never on sale in the United States.

Tonally it is quite satisfying, and it is generally well sung. The phrasing of the first three Caruso recordings of this aria is however faulty. In an attempt to carry over the musical phrase, Caruso breathes as follows :

"Mistico serto di (breath) luce e fior, del (breath) mio pensiero, etc." This is corrected in the 1908 and 1911 versions, to "Mistico serto, (breath) di luce e fior (breath) del mio pensiero etc".

The final B flat is taken pianissimo as marked in the score, but it sounds rather like falsetto although the recording, being rather muddy at this point, makes it uncertain.

GERMANIA (Franchetti) "No non chiuder".

Matrix No. 1788. S/S Cat. No. 52370. D/S Cat. No. D.A. 544.

This record remained on the H.M.V. General catalogue for about seven years after its issue, and then disappeared for some fourteen years to reappear in the No. 2 list in November, 1924, as a double sided disc, (D.A. 544), coupled with the "Studenti Udite" from the same opera, made at the same session. It remained in this list until 1942, in spite of being joined by the two orchestrally accompanied versions of these same titles which Caruso made in 1909. It has now reappeared as V.A. 37 in the Archive Series, and in this form has made its first appearance in the U.S.A.

This is, all in all, my favourite of all the first batch of Milan recordings. The voice is full and rich, and completely under control, and the recording is forward and clear. The music is pleasantly lyrical, and a good original copy is something to cherish.

GERMANIA (Franchetti) "Studenti Udite".

Matrix No. 1782. S/S Cat. No. 52378. D/S Cat. No. 544.

The history of this record is in every respect identical with that of its stable companion just reviewed.

It is interesting to note how often Caruso's recordings are linked as to time with his public appearances. Those who are familiar with Bruno Zirato's Appendix "D" to V. R. Key's "Enrico Caruso" will know how this applies to his operatic recordings, and those of us who heard him at concerts can connect the ballads we heard him sing then, with the dates of his gramophone recordings of them. Caruso made his Zonophone and G & T recordings from "Germania" within a few days of his creation of the role of Lowe, in Milan in March, 1902, and he made his final Germania records in March, 1910, two months after singing in this opera when it made its first appearance in America at the Metropolitan Opera House, New York.

The aria is sung with clarity and vigour and the high tessitura is maintained without effort. It is a splendid example of declamatory singing although musically it is not particularly interesting, and the ending of the record is abrupt and unsatisfactory.

The following ten records were made in Milan on November 12, 1902

LA GIOCONDA (Ponchielli) "Cielo e mar".

Matrix No. 2874. S/S Cat. No. 52417. D/S Cat. No. D.A. 547.

Caruso's first recording of this title was one of the five records made at this session which was issued in February, 1903. After being on the General Catalogue for about seven years, it disappeared from print and emerged nearly fifteen years later on the H.M.V. No. 2 List in 1924 as D.A. 547, backed by the March, 1902 "E lucevan le stelle", and was withdrawn in 1942. It made a welcome return to public life in the Archive Series as V.A. 29, with the same coupling as in 1924. It had been previously issued in U.S.A. under the catalogue numbers 5009 and 91008, but its first appearance there in October, 1903 was a very brief one, for in 1905, following the issue of the Victor recording of the title in May of that year, it was withdrawn.

This is an excellent recording of Caruso's voice when he was only twenty-nine years of age. The high notes ring out clearly, the phrasing is authoritative, and the use of portamento is exemplary. It is more spontaneous than the superb 1905 recording, but lacks the finish of the latter.

AIDA (Verdi) **"Celeste Aida".**

Matrix No. 2873. S/S Cat. No. 52369. D/S Cat. No. D.A. 549.

It is generally agreed that this is a much less desirable rendering of the famous aria than the one made by Caruso eight months previously. Silently substituted under the same catalogue number in the Gramophone and Typewriter Company's Catalogue, it is easily distinguished from the earlier record, not only by its matrix number, but also by its being an abbreviated version of the aria, the final phrases being omitted. It remained on the General Catalogue for about ten years, and then after a disappearance of about eleven years, it re-appeared in the No. 2 List as D.A. 549, with the Fedora aria "Amor ti vieta" on the reverse side, and in this form it remained in print till 1942. It was issued in America under the Victor Numbers 5008 and 91007, but it only remained on the Victor Catalogues from October, 1903 till 1908 when it was superseded by the March, 1908 recording of the aria.

In 1950 it was issued in the Archive Series as V.A. 12, with the very desirable 1904 recording of the first verse of "Una furtiva lagrima" on the reverse side.

As an example of Caruso's singing, it is poor and is also incomplete. It can be avoided safely by all but the curious or omnivorous collector of Caruso's records.

MEFISTOFELE (Boito) **"Dai campi dai prati".**

Matrix No. 2871. S/S Cat. No. 52348. D/S Cat. No. D.A. 550.

This second version of "Dai campi" was re-recorded for exactly the same reason as the "Celeste Aida" which we have just reviewed—namely the collapse of the record made eight months earlier. It is, however, a much more worthy successor to its predecessor than the second "Celeste Aida" is. Though the recording is distinctly less forward, it is quite as beautifully sung, and does not contain a false start. It remained in the General Catalogue for about seven years, and re-appeared as a double sided disc with the issue of the Number 2 Catalogue in 1924, when it was backed by the "Giunto sul passo estremo" as D.A. 550, and was not withdrawn until 1942. It had never been available in America until the Archive Series brought it into light again, on V.A. 7, with the same coupling. As in the case of almost all the 1902 recordings of Caruso, the later pressings show a marked deterioration, and this is shown by a great increase of surface noise, and often by a lack of fulness in the voice itself.

As already remarked, it is a less forward recording than the original one, but it is equally well sung if played at the correct speed. The only obvious difference, is an instrusive "H" on "mister" in the later version, which is not present in the first.

CAVALLERIA RUSTICANA (Mascagni) "Siciliana".

Matrix No. 2876. S/S Cat. No. 52418. D/S Cat. No. D.A. 545.

This was one of the recordings made at this session which was issued in the G & T Supplement of Red Label records in February, 1903. It kept its place in the H.M.V. General Catalogue for about ten years, and in 1924 re-appeared on the Number 2 List as one side of D.A. 545, backed by the 1905 Brindisi from the same opera, and it was not deleted until 1944.

It was issued in the United States in October, 1903, and was on general release from that date until 1904. The Victor Company, not having yet had an opportunity of recording Caruso, put this, and a number of Caruso's Milan recordings on the American market, just before the singer arrived in the United States for the first time in November, 1903. It was withdrawn in the following year to make way for the Victor recording of this same title, made in the February of 1904. It was subsequently again made available here, and in the U.S.A. in the Archive series, issued in October, 1951, backed by the G & T "Vesti la giubba" as V.A. 30.

If played slowly enough, this is a very satisfactory record, although it does not reach the perfection of the final version of 1910. The phrasing is excellent throughout, and the whole is sung with an abandon and a youthful ardour which is most convincing.

PAGLIACCI (Leoncavallo) "Vesti la giubba".

Matrix No. 2875. S/S Cat. No. 52440. D/S Cat. No. D.A. 546.

Caruso's first record of this aria, which more than any other may be called his "signature tune", was issued in February, 1903. After remaining on the General Catalogue for about ten years, and then being withdrawn from circulation for about twelve years, it made its appearance in the Number 2 List in November 1924 as D.A. 546, backed by the same composer's "Mattinata", and was not withdrawn till 1944. It was issued in America (catalogue numbers 5016 and 91014) as so many of the Caruso G & T's were, in October, 1903, to herald the singer's advent to the New World in the following month, but was withdrawn after the Victor recording of the aria in February, 1904. It was again made available in the Archive Series (V.A. 30) backed by the Siciliana from Cavalleria Rusticana.

This is in many ways the best of the Caruso versions of the aria. The approach is fresher than the final version, which sounds sophisticated by comparison, although as an example of legato singing the latter is to be preferred. Dramatically this version is unsurpassed.

"Non t'amo più" (Denza).

Matrix No. 2877. S/S Cat. No. 52441. D/S Cat. No. D.A. 548.

This is another of the records made at this November session which was not issued in England until February, 1903. It remained as did so many of these Milan records, for about ten years on the H.M.V. General Catalogue, and subsequently appeared on the H.M.V. No. 2 List in 1924, as D.A. 548, backed by Tosti's "La Mia Canzone", recorded at the same time, and it remained there till 1941. It was issued in U.S.A. (Victor Catalogue Numbers 5014 and 91013) in October, 1903, but being one of the titles not subsequently recorded by Caruso, it had a longer life than other G & T's not being withdrawn from the Victor Catalogue until 1908. After this it emerged again as one of the Archive series—V.A. 31, with the same coupling as in 1924.

Good Caruso tone and well poised high notes make this a desirable record for all who love the lighter Italian ballads sung to perfection.

"La Mia Canzone" (Tosti).

Matrix No. 2879. S/S Cat. No. 52443. D/S Cat. No. D.A. 548.

The history of this record is exactly the same as that of the one just reviewed, in both England and the United States. Its U.S.A. catalogue numbers before its appearance as an Archive record, were 5011 and 91010.

As a recording of Caruso it is, to our minds, undistinguished in every way. The singing is quite good, indeed very good for anyone but Caruso—but the song is most ordinary.

ADRIANA LECOUVREUR (Cilea) **"No più nobile"**.

Matrix No. 2880. First and only Cat. No. 52419.

This seems to be unquestionably the rarest of all Caruso's G & T records and consequently the one for which collectors are willing to pay the highest price. The unattractiveness of the music would naturally limit the sale of this record, and it was the earliest of all the G & T's to be withdrawn (the March, 1902 "Celeste Aida" and "Dai Campi" were worn out rather than withdrawn) for though it was issued with "Luna Fedel" and the "Fedora" aria later in 1903 than the others recorded at this session, it had disappeared before the March—May, 1907 Catalogue was issued, so that it only had a selling life of about three years. Its attractiveness to collectors is of course enhanced by the fact that the composer plays the piano accompaniment and by the further fact that it is a title which Caruso never recorded again, and from a role which he created. It was never issued in America.

As a recording it is vaguely disappointing. It is undoubtedly beautifully sung, but not more so than the exquisite "Dai Campi" or "Giunto sul passo" or "No non chiuder". The tone is at times strangely similar to De Lucia, and the style is less vigorous and more mannered than in most of Caruso's work. It is indeed a fine example of "Bel canto" if played slowly enough (70-71 r.p.m.). It has the advantage of the composer at the piano, and he seems curiously undecided as to how to round off the excerpt. He wanders on and on, long after the voice has finished, until apparently the engineers decided to call a halt.

FEDORA (Giordano) **"Amor ti vieta"**.

Matrix No. 2872. S/S Cat. No. 52439. D/S Cat. No. D.A. 549.

This record too made its appearance later in 1903 than the earliest issues, and is therefore sometimes wrongly spoken of as a 1903 recording. It remained on the H.M.V. General Catalogue for about seven years, and then after disappearing for about fourteen years it found its way in 1924 into the No. 2 List, backed by the November, 1902 "Celeste Aida", as D.A. 549, and remained there until 1942. It made a welcome second re-appearance in the Archive Series, issued in England in October, 1951, and is backed on V.A. 53 by "Mattinata" (Leoncavallo) and on V.A. 58 by the 1902 G & T rendering of "Il Sogno" from "Manon" (Massenet). This beautiful example of Caruso's singing had never previously been available in America. It has in a special sense an historic interest for it was when he created the role of Loris Ipanoff at the Lirico Milan, on November 17th, 1898 that Caruso's singing of this aria created such a sensation that it proved a turning point in his career. He himself said "after that night contracts descended on me like a heavy rainstorm". Pierre V. R. Key, in his "Enrico Caruso" writes "After the singing of the 'Amor ti vieta' aria, the spark of a new glory was kindled, and the news of it flashed over the telegraph wires to many European cities." One celebrated critic wrote in the course of his comments, "Caruso canto in 'Fedora' e la fe d'oro". (Caruso sang in "Fedora", making it of gold).

This is a most beautiful example of sustained lyrical singing, growing in intensity until the high "A" is reached at the climax. Bonci and De Lucia have both made excellent records of this short aria, and Caruso obviously sang it "con amore". It is superb.

"Luna Fedel" (Denza).

Matrix No. 2882. First and only Cat. No. 52442.

This record with the two just reviewed was issued later in 1903 than the others, but the Gramophone Company's statement to the writer establishes November, 1902 as the date of its recording, and its matrix number confirms this date, as do those of the "Adriana" and "Fedora" titles. It was withdrawn when the March—May, 1907 Catalogue was issued, and has never been on the No. 2 List. Then after a disappearance of about forty-four years, it made its re-appearance in the Archive Series as V.A. 9 with "Hantise d'amour" on the reverse side, and was made available for the first time in America at this late date.

It might well qualify for the title of Caruso's worst record. It is indifferently sung, the music is uninteresting, and the singer makes a bad false entry in the second verse. For the Caruso specialist only!

Recorded September or October, 1903. Milan

PESCATORI DI PERLE (Bizet) **"Mi par d'udir"**.

Matrix No. 268. First Cat. No. 052066.
(German Cat. Nos. 76062 and 85006. As a D/S disc in Germany it was coupled with the 1909 version of the "Flower Song" from Carmen, in French).

This is the first 12 inch record made by Caruso. Doubt has been expressed about the exact date of its recording, some believing it to be a

1902 record, and others dating it in 1904, as it is dated in the H.M.V. Archive List. However, we place it with some confidence as a September or October, 1903 recording, for the reasons we will now give. The Gramophone Company agree that it is not a 1902 record, as no 12 inch records were made by them as early as 1902, but this record cannot be a 1904 one, for it was on the Italian market before the end of 1903, and Mr. Robert Bauer has found it in the Catalogue of January 1st, 1904, and he says "the label shows undoubtedly a 1903 recording". A review of Caruso's singing engagements during 1903 almost ties us to the acceptance of September or October as the time of recording. This record remained on the H.M.V. General Catalogue for about thirteen years but for some reason it never found its way into the No. 2 List, and it remained in retirement after the appearance of the French version made in December, 1916 until its re-appearance in the Archive Series in 1951 on V.B. 44, backed by the 1904 recording of the second stanza of the famous aria from "L'Elisir d'amore". But though this describes its history as a general release, it formed, as is well known to collectors, one side of the disc issued in 1936, in America by the International Record Collectors' Club (No. 61A) in conjunction with the Victor Company, the reverse side of which contained the Caruso-Farrar duet from the first act of Puccini's "La Bohème."

This first 12 inch recording of Caruso is in many ways interesting. The difficult phrasing and the high tessitura are well managed, but the final phrase, which is not in the score, includes an obvious falsetto high note, which Caruso avoids in his 1911 recording.

Recorded April, 1904. Milan

"Mattinata" (Leoncavallo).

> Matrix No. 2181. S/S Cat. No. 52034. D/S Cat. No. D.A. 546. German Cat. No. 74511.

This is the last of the historic Milan recordings, and is the only one made by Caruso after he had begun to record for the Victor Company, and was recorded by him almost immediately after his return to Europe at the close of his first season at the Metropolitan Opera, New York. As is well known, the composer went with Caruso to the Hotel Continental, Milan, and acted as his accompanist. Neither Mr. F. W. Gaisberg nor his brother were present on this occasion, and the recording was done by Mr. W. S. Derby. As far as we have been able to ascertain, the first announcement of this record in England was made in the July, 1904 issue of the "Gramophone News", which then corresponded to "The Voice" of later days, but it seems to have been available to the Italian public as early as in May of that year. The following quotation from "The Gramophone News" will be of interest to all who like to know about the histories of these early records. "Caruso's new record. Ruggiero Leoncavallo, the famous Italian composer has specially written and composed a song for the Gramophone and Typewriter Co. Ltd., entitled 'Mattinata' ('Tis the day) No. R.L. 52034. We engaged Cav. Caruso to sing the above record, published at ten shillings. By special command Caruso sang before their Majesties the King and Queen at Buckingham Palace, when the Austrian Archduke was in England. By request, the great Italian tenor sang our song ("Mattinata") accompanied by Mr. Landon Ronald. Cavalier Caruso is singing this song at all his social functions this season". As was the case with so many of the Milans, this record remained on the H.M.V. General Catalogue for about ten years, was then withdrawn to re-appear in 1924 on the No. 2 List as D.A. 546, backed by the Milan "Vesti la Giubba" where it held its place till 1946. This record had never been on general release in U.S.A. till its appearance in the Archive Series on V.A. 32, where it is backed by the 1904 Victor recording of "Il sogno" from Massenet's "Manon", and on V.A. 53 where it is coupled with the 1902 "Fedora" aria. The non issue of this attractive record in America was presumably due to the Victor Company having begun to record Caruso before this recording was made. The authors think this record reproduces best at a higher speed— about 77—than other Milan records.

This is, musically speaking, a pleasing if ordinary record. The singing is convincing, and at the same time pleasantly lyrical, and the quality of the recording is more like that of the 1902 series than the Victors of 1904.

THE VICTOR RECORDS

EXCEPT for "Mattinata", Caruso never made a record for any company other than the Victor Company, after making his first Victor records in New York, in Room No. 826 of the Carnegie Hall on February 1st, 1904. Henceforth America was to be the only scene of his recording activities and we have left behind us, as it were, the obscurities and uncertainties which surround so many of those early European recordings. The historian of Caruso's records may be thankful that unlike some famous singers he never complicated the problem of presenting a clear picture of his recorded legacy by transferring his affections to other companies in spite of strong inducements held out to him to do so. A special interest belongs to Caruso's early Victors, for it is generally agreed that they were the records made in his greatest years. From 1904 to 1907 he was becoming an even greater singer than he had been and was learning how to employ to the full the resources of his marvellous organ, nor till after 1907 did his voice lose anything of its lyric beauty. In addition to this, those were the years when the recording of the human voice was at last coming into its own, for it was Caruso's good fortune that the recorder's art had, so to speak, caught up to its job before the period of his fullest vocal glory had begun to pass away.

The ten records made on February 1st, 1904 have a character of their own though they are not all equally successful. They are forward in tone and sound best when played at a speed of about 80 r.p.m. None of them we think, preserves quite as much beauty as the 1905 ones do, but as specimens of his singing they are not inferior to any records he ever made for it was evidently determined at this session that nothing should be lost through the singer not being given plenty of time. This is perhaps specially noticeable in his renderings of the "Aida" and "L'Elisir d'amore" numbers, but it is evident in all the results of this first Victor session. As a result, these records, and the ones published in the following year, show Caruso in his most classical mood. His former exuberance is now gone, and he seems determined to

23

show his technical mastery of his instrument. For this reason alone they are most valuable documents.

The following ten records were made in New York on February 1st, 1904

RIGOLETTO (Verdi) **"Questa o quella".**

> Matrix No. 994. First Victor S/S Cat. No. 81025. Victor D/S Cat. No. 522B.

In its double sided form it was coupled with the "La donna è mobile" made at the same session. This is one of the four records made at this session which has so far never appeared in any English catalogue, but has the European Catalogue number 2-52480. It was on general sale in the United States from April, 1904 until 1924.

As an interpretation it sounds lifeless compared with either the 1902 or 1908 version. It is however most carefully sung, and the "A" flats are taken without any sense of effort. One feels, however, that Caruso was singing to orders. His natural sparkle is not here, and the record is smooth but uninteresting.

RIGOLETTO (Verdi) **"La donna è mobile".**

> Matrix No. 995. First Victor S/S Cat. No. 81026. Victor D/S Cat. No. 522A. English S/S Cat. No. 52062.

This record made its appearance in England soon after it was recorded, but only remained on the H.M.V. General List for about three years, and then disappeared entirely, never finding a place in the No. 2 List. It was available in the United States from April, 1904 until 1924.

Though better than the "Questa o quella", this record also lacks the rhythmic snap and the brilliance of the 1908 version. It is again carefully sung, with a delightful modulation of the voice on "Muta d'accento", while the cadenza is sung with wonderful agility. The final notes sound lifeless, and the high "B" at the close is not quite in the centre. Again there is a feeling of restraint.

L'ELISIR D'AMORE (Donizetti) **"Una furtiva lagrima".**

> Matrix No. B996. First Victor Cat. No. 81027. Later Victor Cat. No. 930. English Cat. No. 52065. (10 inch record, first stanza only). Archive Series V.Á.12. (for notes see below following record).

24

L'ELISIR D'AMORE (Donizetti) "Un solo istante i palpiti".

Matrix No. C996. First and only Victor Cat. No. 85021. English Cat. No. 052073 (12 inch record, second stanza only). Archive Series V.B.16 and V.B.44.

The devotion of these two discs to the recording of this famous aria is evidence for what we have written about the determination shown by the engineers during this session, that Caruso should not be hurried. The result is generally agreed to be one of the finest specimens of bel canto ever recorded. These two records remained on the H.M.V. General Catalogue for about eight years, and were then withdrawn to make way for the orchestra accompanied version of the aria which Caruso recorded in December, 1911. These discs were never listed in the No. 2 Catalogue, which made their appearance in the October, 1951 Archive Series a most welcome one. After their issue in America in April, 1904, the one giving the first stanza remained in print until 1919, but the twelve inch disc was withdrawn in 1907.

These two records must be dealt with together. The 10 inch disc contains the first verse, and the 12 inch one the second. The recording is good for the period, and more forward than in some of the series. The singing and interpretation are models of classical perfection. In the first verse there is a perfectly judged climax on the words "Io vo'— m'ama si m'ama" followed by an equally fine diminuendo. The second verse is a tour de force, the long messa di voce on "ah—cielo" being particularly fine. The cadenza shows off the remarkable agility of Caruso's voice. All in all, these two records might well be chosen as Caruso's most perfect technical achievement, for he has plenty of time to spread himself. Records such as the unsurpassed "O Paradiso" may be equally unique, in that no other singer since the inception of recording has approached them, but the classical simplicity and purity of style as shown in these two 1904 discs places them in a class apart.

AIDA (Verdi) "Celeste Aida".

Matrix No. 997. First and only Victor Cat. No. 85022. Only H.M.V. Cat. No. 052074.

This, the first Caruso recording of this aria on a 12 inch disc, remained on the H.M.V. Catalogue until 1922, in spite of the 1908 and 1911 recordings of the title. But when withdrawn from the General Catalogue, it disappeared altogether, never finding its way into the No. 2 List. It is sung more slowly than the other four versions. In America this record was available from April, 1904 until 1909.

This recording shows similar phrasing to the 1902 versions, and beautifully managed portamenti, while the final "B" flat is sung as marked in the score. The main objections are muddy recording, and a really fierce surface noise. In addition there is little of the tremendous intensity which we associate with Caruso at his finest, perhaps the recording is to blame, or was he setting out to make a record which showed off his vocal technique rather than his interpretative powers?

TOSCA (Puccini) "E lucevan le stelle".

> Matrix No. 998. Victor S/S Cat. No. 81028. Later D/S Cat. No. 523B. European S/S Cat. No. 52063, and D/S Cat. No. D.A. 125.

This record was never available in England till the issue of the Archive Series in 1951, when it appeared on V.A. 34 (backed by the 1904 recording of "Recondita Armonia") but it was on the Continental H.M.V. List for many years and in its double sided form survived the outbreak of the Second World War. In the United States it was available from April, 1904 until 1924.

Again the insistence on orthodox singing and technical perfection are noteworthy. Possibly the emphasis on these matters detracts in some way from the dramatic interpretation. The high "A" on "disciogliea dai veli" is moulded and lingered over in a way which excites our admiration for the singer's immense resources, and is entirely in keeping with the composer's instructions. The one blemish is the sob at the end, which is ludicrous as recorded.

TOSCA (Puccini) "Recondita Armonia".

> Matrix No. 999. First Victor Cat. No. 81029. H.M.V. Cat. No. 52191.

This is Caruso's first recording of this aria, and it remained on the H.M.V. General Catalogue for about six years and then, following the issue of the same title made by Caruso in November, 1909, it disappeared altogether from the Gramophone Company's lists until its reappearance in October, 1951, in the Archive Series on V.A. 34, backed by the recording just reviewed. In America it was available from April, 1904 until 1909.

This is one of the best of the 1904 series, and the ease and grace of the singing are a revelation. This aria appears to have been a favourite of Caruso's, and he certainly sings the sweeping phrases con amore. The final passage "ah il mio sol pensier sei tu, Tosca sei tu" is thrilling as the voice rises and falls effortlessly finally reaching a triumphant B flat.

CAVALLERIA RUSTICANA (Mascagni) **"Siciliana"**.

Matrix No. 1,000. Victor S/S Cat. No. 81030. D/S Cat. No. 521B. H.M.V. S/S Cat. No. 52064. German Cat. No. 80081.

This is another of Caruso's 1904 records which has never so far been made available in England. It remained on the Victor Catalogue from April, 1904 until 1924.

It is satisfactory without being in any way outstanding, compared with the best of the years' issues. In this case, the final attempt of 1909 was to eclipse the earlier versions.

MANON (Massenet) **"Chiudo gli occhi"** (Il sogno).

Matrix No. 1001. First Victor Cat. No. 81031. D/S Cat. No. 523A. H.M.V. S/S Cat. No. 2-52479. H.M.V. D/S Cat. No. D.A. 125. German Cat. Nos. 74516 and 80005.

Here is another of the records made at this session which was never on any English catalogue till the appearance of the Archive Series in October, 1951, when it was listed as V.A. 32 backed by "Mattinata". It had, however, a long history in America, where it was available from April, 1904 until 1924, and it was also procurable on the Continent of Europe for many years after its issue. (It was still listed in the Italian catalogue for 1953).

Fine recording, a wonderful control of emission, and an admirable legato, make this one of Caruso's finest discs. The mezza voce is firm and always masculine, and yet of a velvety softness and a caressing warmth. The piano accompaniment seems less odd in this record than in most of the early ones, and is not unsuitable as a substitute for the delicate tracery of the strings, in the full score.

I PAGLIACCI (Leoncavallo) **"Vesti la giubba"**.

Matrix No. 1002. First Victor Cat. No. 81032. Victor D/S Cat. No. 930. H.M.V. S/S Cat. No. 52066.

This record was only retained in the H.M.V. General Catalogue for about two years. The appearance of the final recording of the title was in March, 1907, and this was the signal for the 1904 recording's disappearance from all English catalogues. In America it was on general release from April, 1904 until 1910.

This is the least effective of the three versions to be handed down to us. The vocal tone sounds constricted, and altogether the singing is not outstanding for Caruso. The tremendous resonance of the passage "Ridi Pagliaccio" in the orchestral version is missing, and the tessitura shows signs of causing some discomfort. The phrasing is, as usual intelligent, and musically sound.

The five records which follow are, we think, better reproductions of Caruso's voice than are the 1904 ones, and perhaps the best as till then made. But to be heard to the fullest advantage they should not be played at a speed above 77. This is the last session at which the piano was the only instrument employed for accompaniment. Caruso here breaks fresh ground, none of these titles having been previously recorded by him. They were all on the H.M.V. General Catalogue soon after they were recorded.

The following five records were made in New York on February 27, 1905

CAVALLERIA RUSTICANA (Mascagni) **"Viva il vino"** (Brindisi).

> Matrix No. 2344. First Victor Cat. No. 81062. Victor D/S Cat. No. 521A. H.M.V. S/S Cat. No. 52193. D/S Cat. No. D.A.545. German Cat. Nos. 74513 and 80005.

The only ten inch record made at this session, it, together with the Don Pasquale Serenade, retained its place on the H.M.V. General Catalogue until the appearance of the No. 2 List in 1924, in which it appeared in double sided form, backed by the November, 1902 "Siciliana". (In the U.S.A. it was coupled with the 1904 "Siciliana"). It was not withdrawn from the No. 2 List until 1944 and it then reappeared in 1951, in the Archive Series as V.A. 33, coupled with the "Manon Lescaut" aria "Donna non vidi mai" made by Caruso in February, 1913.

This contains a magnificent example of Caruso's extraordinary breath control, and finishes with one of the worst high notes he ever recorded. It sounds very much like falsetto, and is quite unnecessary as an addition to the score. A worthwhile record for its many virtues despite dull recording.

DON PASQUALE (Donizetti) **"Com'è gentil"**.

> Matrix No. 2340. First Victor Cat. No. 85048. Victor D/S Cat. No. 6036A. H.M.V. S/S Cat. No. 052086. D/S Cat. No. D.B. 159.

This record had exactly the same history in England as the Cavalleria Rusticana record just reviewed except that it was withdrawn a year earlier—1943—from the No. 2 List where for nearly twenty years it was coupled with the 1906 recording of the romance from Marta. In the U.S.A. it was available from May, 1905 until 1924, and in its double sided form was backed by the rendering of "Cielo e mar" which Caruso made on the same day. It re-appeared in 1951 in the Archive series as V.B. 55 backed by the piano accompanied 1914 version of "La Partida".

A lovely aria, well recorded for its age, and sung throughout in a most delicious mezza voce. The control and restraint are superb, and so are the faultless turns. The use of the portamento is unerring, and the whole disc is one to treasure.

CARMEN (Bizet) "Il fior che avevi a me tu dato".

Matrix No. 2341. Victor S/S Cat. No. 85049. H.M.V. S/S Cat. No. 052087. (It was never issued in double sided form either in this country or America until the appearance of the Archive series).

This beautiful record only remained on the H.M.V. Catalogue for about five years and then completely disappeared until 1951, so that its appearance as V.B. 57 where it was coupled with the 1905 Huguenots aria, was a most welcome one. Fortunately this is one of the shells which shows no sign of deterioration. In America this record had a comparatively brief history, only being listed in the Victor Catalogue from May, 1905 until 1909.

The first recording of this aria, and in many ways the best. The high notes have an unbelievable ease, and the voice itself has never sounded more beautiful, being of a velvety quality combined with a youthful freshness. The final B flat might have been held a fraction of a second longer, but really the disc as a whole calls for unstinted praise. No other singer who recorded this aria has approached so near to perfection.

GLI UGONOTTI (Meyerbeer) "Bianca al par di neve alpina".

Matrix No. 2342. Victor S/S Cat. No. 85056. H.M.V. S/S Cat. No. 052088.

This, like the Carmen record just reviewed was never issued in double sided form till its 1951 appearance in the Archive Series as V.B. 57. In its single sided form it only retained its place in the H.M.V. General Catalogue for about five years. As is well known, both this title and the Flower Song were re-recorded by Caruso in November, 1909, and the appearance of these final recordings of the two titles led to the speedy disappearance of their 1905 predecessors. In U.S.A. it was available from May, 1905 until 1909. It re-appeared there in the counterpart of the H.M.V. No. 2 List, which was issued by Victor in 1927.

This record is a worthy companion to the Carmen aria just reviewed. The uncanny control of the voice, the mezza voce, the ringing head notes are all here in full measure, and make this a model of bel canto singing.

LA GIOCONDA (Ponchielli) "Cielo e mar".

Matrix No. 2343. Victor S/S Cat. No. 85055. Victor D/S Cat. No. 6036B. H.M.V. S/S Cat. No. 052089. H.M.V. D/S Cat. No. D.B.113.

This record had a history more worthy of its merits than some of the others made at this session. Perhaps it is, as a reproduction of Caruso's voice just a shade ahead of any of the other four, excellent as they all are. It remained on the H.M.V. General List until Caruso made his third and final recording of the aria in 1910, and then after having vanished for about fourteen years, it came to life on the No. 2 List as D.B. 113, backed by "Che gelida manina" (La Bohème), where it remained until 1946, outliving its 1910 successor by about four years. In the U.S.A., when it appeared in double sided form, it was backed by the "Don Pasquale" aria made at the same session and was on general release from May, 1905 until 1924.

It is difficult to say more of this series without undue repetition. Suffice it to add that Caruso was at the height of his powers when singing this aria. The voice soars again and again with a freedom and a beauty which are unique among tenors of this century.

The following five records were made in New York on February 11th, 1906

This is, of course, a most important session and we should be very thankful for its results, but the fact that these were the first records made by Caruso with orchestral accompaniment may have had some effect upon the recording of his voice. Perhaps just from the standpoint of recording they do not on the whole show the advance upon those of the previous twelve months that might have been expected at this time when recording technique was making such a rapid advance. Only in the "Marta" and "La Favorita" arias does the recording seem as good as might have been hoped. We are now passing from the time of Caruso's "historic" records and leaving behind the uncertainties which becloud the histories of these, and we are also coming to the time when we shall find that the issue in this country of Caruso's records did not always follow as closely as hitherto their recording in America. So much did this ultimately become the case that though his final session took place eleven months before his death, no less than twenty-four of his records were posthumously issued during the next nine years.

IL TROVATORE (Verdi) "Di quella pira".

> Matrix No. 3103. Victor S/S Cat. No. 87001. Victor D/S Cat. Nos. 512 and 3031. H.M.V. S/S Cat. No. 2-52489. D/S Cat. No. D.A. 113. German Cat. Nos. 74518 and 80007, backed by the final rendering of "La Donna è mobile".

This record, issued in England soon after its recording remained on the General Catalogue till after Caruso's death and was then transferred to the No. 2 List (coupled with Leoncavallo's "Lasciati amar") and was not deleted till 1945. In America this record as 512, was backed by the "Ballo in Maschera" aria "Dì tu se fedele" and as 3031 by the Brindisi duet from "La Traviata" with Gluck, and was available from May, 1906 until 1930. Caruso retained "Il Trovatore" in his repertoire for a surprisingly short period, singing it for the first time in New York in February, 1908 and for the last time in January, 1909 at the Academy of Music in Philadelphia. It will be noticed that it was during those two years that three of his "Il Trovatore" records were made.

This aria is not too well recorded and as a result the quality of his voice suffers. The high "C's" sound a trifle pinched, and there is some sign of strain. Although Tamagno's version is less perfect technically, I prefer his rendering in this case, owing to its greater freedom.

FAUST (Gounod) "Salut demeure chaste et pure".

> Matrix No. 3102. Victor S/S Cat. No. 88003. Victor D/S Cat. No. 6004. H.M.V. S/S Cat. No. 032030. H.M.V. D/S Cat. No. D.K. 116. German Cat. Nos. 76013 and 85004, reverse side "Ah fuyez douce image" (Manon).

Caruso's first record not sung in Italian was issued here soon after being recorded and it kept its place in the General Catalogue till the issue of the No. 2 List in the autumn of 1924 to which it was then transferred as D.K. 116, having on its reverse side the duet with Ancona from the Pearl Fishers, "Del tempio al limitar". It was deleted from the No. 2 List in 1946. In the U.S.A. it was coupled with

31

the French version of the Flower Song from Carmen, recorded in November, 1909, and was available from May, 1906 until 1933.

I find this a most disappointing record. Possibly this is due to the fact that it is Caruso's first recording in French. Anyhow the vocal quality is not as fine as usual, the style is uncertain, and even the intonation causes occasional misgivings. This disc does Caruso considerably less than justice.

LA FAVORITA (Donizetti) "Spirito gentil".

Matrix No. 3104. Victor S/S Cat. No. 88004. D/S Cat. No. 6005. H.M.V. S/S Cat. No. 052120. H.M.V. D/S Cat. No. D.B. 129. German Cat. Nos. 76064 and 85010.

The history of this record in this country is exactly similar to that of the one just reviewed, except that it was withdrawn from the H.M.V. No. 2 List in 1942. As D.B. 129 it was coupled with Tosti's "Ideale" but in U.S.A. where it was on the Victor Catalogues from May, 1906 until 1933, it had on its reverse side the November, 1909 version of the Huguenot's aria "Bianca al par". In Germany it was backed by the first rendering of "In terra solo" from "Don Sebastiano". It was also issued in America in later years as one side of Victor Heritage 15-1036.

This is my favourite recording of the aria. No one else has succeeded in maintaining so perfect a legato, or of suggesting so successfully the reflective nature of the scene. Bonci over dramatises the aria by paying too much attention to the colouring of individual words and phrases, at the expense of the aria as a whole, and Gigli, in his excellent pre-electric recording, lacks the perfect legato. Caruso's breathing is here phenomenal, and the high "C" is beautifully placed and held. This is a model for all students of bel canto.

MARTA (Flotow) "M'appari tutt' amor".

Matrix No. 3100. 1 S/S and only Victor Cat. No. 88001. H.M.V. S/S Cat. No. 052121. D/S Cat. No. D.B. 159. German Cat. Nos. 76065 and 85011.

This record retained its place in the H.M.V. General Catalogue until the advent of the No. 2 List in 1924, on which it was coupled with the Serenade from "Don Pasquale", and was not deleted before 1943. This is, of course, not the rendering from which the electrically re-recorded version derives. In U.S.A. it was originally listed from May 1906 until 1917, and then, as noted in the review of "Spirito Gentil" it was re-issued in the Heritage Series as 15-1036. In Germany it had the 1909 rendering of the Huguenots Romance on the reverse side.

This is the most beautiful singing, although the recording sounds a trifle constrained. The legato is perfect, and the long sustained phrasing a joy to the connoisseur. Caruso eases the approach to the high "B" flat at the close, by inserting a preliminary "ah", singing "Ah, si morro" and not "Si morro" as in the score.

LA BOHEME (Puccini) **"Che gelida manina".**

Matrix No. 3101. Victor S/S Cat. No. 88002. D/S Cat. No. 6003. H.M.V. S/S Cat. No. 052122. D/S Cat. No. D.B. 113. German Cat. Nos. 76066 and 85012.

This record has the same long and uneventful history as those we have just reviewed. It only left the General Catalogue for the comparative obscurity of the No. 2 List in 1924, with the 1905 "Cielo e mar" on the reverse side, and was not deleted from it until 1946. In America where it was available from May, 1906 until 1940, as 6003, it was backed by Buzzi Pecchia's "Lolita". In Germany, as a double sided record, it had the orchestrally accompanied rendering of "Una furtiva lagrima" on the reverse side.

The interpretation grows on one. At first it sounds slightly hesitant, compared with Gigli's superb version, but careful consideration of the aria makes one realize that Caruso does more than give us fine singing. The aria should be in the nature of an improvisation, and it is just this that the singer suggests. The high "C" is most beautifully taken, and it is difficult to realize that Caruso, in his early days, asked Puccini to excuse him from singing this note. All in all, this is a very fine version.

Recorded March 13th, 1906, New York

LA FORZA DEL DESTINO (Verdi) **"Solenne in quest'ora"** (with Scotti).

Matrix No. 3179. Victor S/S Cat. No. 89001. D/S Cat. No. 8000. H.M.V. S/S Cat. No. 054070. D/S Cat. No. D.M. 105. German Cat. No. 78510.

This record, which was Caruso's first concerted record, and remained his favourite duet record to the end of his life, was released here soon after its recording and remained on the General Catalogue till the holocaust of 1946 swept it and all Caruso's other concerted numbers from the catalogue. In this country it was coupled, in its double sided form, with the duet with Scotti from "La Bohème", "O Mimi tu piu non torni" as it also was as a Victor record. In America it was on general release from June 1906 until 1948.

This contains some very lovely singing on the part of both artistes, and Caruso's high notes are beautifully poised, and sufficiently light to suggest the wounded Don Alvaro better than most other tenors have done. There is an obvious difficulty in the interpretation of this duet. If the tenor sings softly enough to suggest a dying man, then the balance between the two voices will be faulty from a musical point of view. It is no use stating that this version offers an easy solution of this difficulty, but it does contain some very fine singing.

The following two records were made in New York on December 30th, 1906

"Ideale" (Tosti).

> Matrix No. 4162. Victor S/S Cat. No. 88049. D/S Cat. No. 6019. H.M.V. S/S Cat. No. 052154. D/S Cat. No. D.B. 129. German Cat. Nos. 76071 and 85003.

This record kept its place on the General Catalogue for about seventeen years and was then transferred to the No. 2 List (Coupled with "Spirito Gentil") and was deleted in 1942. In America it was coupled with "Fenesta che lucive" and was available from March, 1907 until 1924. As a German double sided disc, it had Bizet's "Agnus Dei" on the reverse side.

Tosti knew how to write for the voice, and Caruso knew how to sing songs like this. The beginning of the aria shows off the lovely quality of his medium register, and there is a delightful mezza voce finish. The only criticism to offer, is that there is a rather explosive release from one high note. This apart, the record is a model.

"Triste Ritorno" (Barthelemy).

> Matrix No. 4159. Victor S/S Cat. No. 88048. D/S Cat. No. 6030. H.M.V. S/S Cat. No. 052153. D/S Cat. No. D.B. 140. German Cat. Nos. 76070 and 85005.

This record remained on the H.M.V. General List till the first issue on the No. 2 List, in November, 1924, when it took its place as D.B. 140. with "Fenesta che lucive" on the reverse side, and was deleted in 1941. As a Victor double sided disc, it was coupled with "Uocchi celeste" and was available from March, 1907 until 1927. In Germany it had "Adorables tourments" on the reverse side.

I must confess that many Italian songs do not appeal to me particularly, as I consider that their musical content is not sufficient to justify their appearance on records. However, Caruso's singing of this example makes it well worth hearing, despite the fact that the recording is not up to the others of this session.

The following two records were made in New York on February 20th, 1907

RIGOLETTO (Verdi) **"Bella figlia dell'amore"** (with Abbott, Homer & Scotti).

> Matrix No. 4259. Victor S/S Cat. No. 96000. D/S Cat. No. 10011. H.M.V. S/S Cat. No. 054117. D/S Cat. No. D.O. 100. German Cat. No. 79000.

This record was issued in England shortly after its recording and kept its place on the H.M.V. General Catalogue till 1946. After 1923 it was coupled with the duel trio from Faust, (with Scotti and Journet) and in America, where it was available from March, 1907 until 1924, its coupling was the same. It was apparently never issued in Germany as a double sided record.

This recording is noteworthy for Caruso's magnificent singing of the introductory tenor solo. From this point of view I consider it the best of the four versions in which Caruso takes part, although all have their points. It is the most purely lyrical version, and sung with more legato than any of the others. The word "palpitar" on the phrase rising to the high B flat is sung without interruption, whereas in the recording of February, 1908 a breath is taken after the first note and the rest of the ascending passage is sung on "ah". Abbott's singing is competent, and Homer and Scotti are quite satisfactory when they can be heard. As a concerted recording, I do not consider this, or any other recorded version of the great quartet to be entirely satisfactory, but for the student of singing there is much to be learnt from Caruso's part as reproduced on this disc.

L'AFRICANA (Meyerbeer) **"O Paradiso"**.

> Matrix No. 4160. Victor S/S Cat. No. 88054. D/S Cat. No. 6007. H.M.V. S/S Cat. No. 052157. D/S Cat. No. D.B. 117. German Cat. Nos. 76072 and 85015.

This record kept its place on the H.M.V. General Catalogue for over 43 years, but alas, is due for deletion almost as these words are being written, nothing being left, but the much inferior electrical reproduction taken from this great record. In its double sided form it was coupled in England with the Italian version of the Flower Song from "Carmen",

35

made in 1909, as it was also, as a Victor issue, and as a German issue. It was on general release in U.S.A. from March, 1907 until 1930.

This is singing in the grand manner. At last the recording does something like justice to the great tenor, and as yet there is no deterioration in his voice. The result is another tour de force. The phrasing is easy and fluid, the high notes ring out as never before, and there is an air of authority which makes this the finest version of the aria so far recorded. Something happens on the very last note. Whether it is the fault of the singer or the recorder it is difficult to say, but in any case, it is a trifling defect in such a magnificent record.

The following five records were made in New York in March, 1907

This session is very important, for it is perhaps the most valuable in its results of any in which Caruso ever took part. The recording has now become more or less standardised, and broadly speaking does as much justice to his voice as in subsequent sessions, while the beauty of that voice is still untarnished. It is not until the next session, ten months later, that we notice the first signs of the trouble which was to lead to the operation on the singer's vocal chords, after which, though it remained a magnificent voice, something had gone from Caruso's singing which never came back again.

I PAGLIACCI (Leoncavallo) **"Vesti la giubba"**. Recorded March 17th, 1907
> Matrix No. 4317. Victor S/S Cat. No. 88061. D/S Cat. No. 6001. H.M.V. S/S Cat. No. 052159. D/S Cat. No. D.B. 111. German Cat. Nos. 76074 and 85017.

Issued with all expedition, soon after its recording, this final record of the aria which above all others is associated with Caruso's name, has so far survived the vicissitudes of the years, and in 1951 was one of the few original Caruso records still on the H.M.V. General Catalogue. After 1923 it took its place in double sided form with "No, Pagliaccio non son" on the reverse side. As a Victor record it was available from July, 1907 until 1953, and had the same coupling, as it also had in Germany. It has, as is well known, appeared in America in company with non Caruso recordings.

This is probably the most famous record Caruso ever made, and it certainly appears to have been his "best seller" by the frequency with which copies turn up. In its way, it is of course stupendous, and the ease with which the climax, "sul tuo amore infranto" is carried in one breath, with majestic resonance and stupendous power, is amazing. No other tenor could have given us this, and yet, in some ways I do not think that this is representative of the best in Caruso's art. For the general public, this record is almost Caruso's "signature tune", but the voice lacks the sensuous beauty of other records of this date. It is a great voice, but it is "all out", and gives me less pleasure than when the great tenor is singing well within himself.

ANDREA CHENIER (Giordano) **"Un di, all'azzurro"**. Recorded March 17th, 1907.

> Matrix No. 4316. Victor S/S Cat. No. 88060. D/S Cat. No. 6008. H.M.V. S/S Cat. No. 052158. D/S Cat. No. D.B. 700. German Cat. Nos. 76073 and 85016.

This record retained its place in the H.M.V. Catalogue till 1924, when, though unsurpassed by any record Caruso ever made, it was relegated to the comparative obscurity of the No. 2 List, where it remained until its deletion in 1942. As D.B. 700 it was backed by "In terra solo" from Don Sebastiano, but as a Victor double sided record it was coupled with the "Addio all madre" from "Cavalleria Rusticana", and was available from March, 1907 until 1933. In Germany it was coupled with the final "Cielo e mar".

This is one of my great favourites among all Caruso's recordings. The matchless fire, the perfect phrasing, the consummate technique are all employed in this unsurpassed rendering. It is lyrical singing of the very highest order, and the way the great tenor rises effortlessly, without a preliminary breath to the high B flats, is an example of the mastery which placed him in a class by himself. This record is in every way equal to the much better known "O Paradiso" which Caruso recorded a month previously.

LA BOHEME (Puccini) **"A Mimi tu più non torni"** (with Scotti). Recorded March 17th, 1907.

> Matrix No. 4315. Victor S/S Cat. No. 89006. D/S Cat. No. 8000. H.M.V. S/S Cat. No. 054127. D/S Cat. No. D.M. 105. German Cat. Nos. 78511 and 78510.

This record, issued in England soon after its recording in New York, remained on the H.M.V. General Catalogue till 1946. After 1923 it was coupled with the "Forza del Destino" duet, made a year previously. In America it had the same coupling and was available from

May, 1907 until 1948. As a German disc, its coupling was the same as here and in U.S.A.

To opera goers of half a century ago, the names of Caruso, Melba and Scotti were sure to crop up if "La Bohème" was mentioned, and this record of the famous duet from the last act will not disappoint those who are too young to have heard the artists in the flesh. Scotti's voice is refined and mellow, while Caruso is in magnificent form. His head notes are beautifully taken, without any sense of restriction, and the typical Puccini phrases are floated on the breath with an incomparable beauty of tone, and with an appropriate tinge of melancholy in the timbre. This is a delightful record.

I PESCATORI DI PERLE (Bizet) "Del tempio al limitar" (with Ancona). Recorded March 24th, 1907.

> Matrix No. 4327. Victor S/S Cat. No. 89007. D/S Cat. No. 8036. H.M.V. S/S Cat. No. 054134. D/S Cat. No. D.K. 116. German Cat. No. 78513.

Another record to be issued as was usually the case in those early days, soon after its recording, it remained on the H.M.V. General Catalogue until 1946. After 1923 it appeared in the H.M.V. No. 2 List as D.K. 116, backed by the 1906 "Salut demeure", but as a Victor record it was coupled with the "Don Carlos" duet made with Scotti in 1912, and this was available in U.S.A. from June 1907 until 1928. In Germany it was backed by the "Otello" Brindisi, sung by Amato and Setti.

Still another wonderful example of Caruso's art, and on this occasion he is well matched by Ancona's polished singing of the baritone part. This is a most welcome record of a beautiful duet, and the singing is fresh and easy. Caruso's high notes are exquisite, and are perfectly placed.

Altogether March, 1907 was in many ways his peak period for recording, since the apparatus was now able to catch some of the beauty of the voice which was still in its prime.

LA BOHEME (Puccini) "O soave fanciulla" (with Melba). Recorded March 24th, 1907.

> Matrix No. 4326. Victor S/S Cat. No. 95200. H.M.V. S/S Cat. No. 054129.

Available here soon after its recording in New York, this record remained on the H.M.V. General List until 1946. Neither in England nor in America has this record ever been issued except in single sided form, but in Germany in double sided form it was backed by the 1908 "Celeste Aida". It was available in America from March, 1907 until 1927.

Once again Caruso is in his most entrancing mood, and the voice of Melba, though inadequately recorded, contrasts well with the warm easy tones of the tenor. As a record of the duet, this is not wholly satisfying, as the balance is not all that could be desired, although Melba's final top C rings out well and true, but as a record of Caruso's voice, there are few which could beat it.

The following three records were made in New York on January 10th, 1908

"Adorables tourments" (Caruso-Barthelemy).

> Matrix No. 5009. Victor S/S Cat. No. 88115. D/S Cat. No. 6006. H.M.V. S/S Cat. No. 032070. D/S Cat. No. D.B. 116. German Cat. Nos. 76014 and 85005.

This record was available in England soon after it was recorded and remained on the H.M.V. General Catalogue till 1923, and then in double sided form it retained its place till 1941. Caruso is credited with being the author of the words, his friend and coach Richard Barthelemy being the composer. As D.B. 116, it was coupled with the "Chanson de Juin", as it was in America, where it was available from May, 1908 until 1927. As a German disc, it was backed by the "Triste Ritorno" also composed by Barthelemy.

My own reaction to this record is that it is a waste of wax, a waste of talent, and a waste of time. Caruso had recorded trifles before, but they were always typical Italian and Neapolitan canzonettas. The present example is an attempt at a purely commercial pot-boiler which has not quite "come off".

The voice is quite good, but the whole result is a pathetic waste of Caruso's voice and talents when they were in their prime.

DON SEBASTIANO (Donizetti) **"In terra solo"**.

> Matrix No. 5008. Victor S/S Cat. No. 88106. D/S Cat. No. 6014. H.M.V. S/S Cat. No. 052209. D/S Cat. No. D.B. 700. German Cat. Nos. 76078 and 85010.

This record was issued in England in June 1908, and remained on the H.M.V. General Catalogue until 1923, when it was relegated to the No. 2 List and finally deleted in 1942. As D.B. 700 it was coupled with the

Andrea Chenier "Un di all' azzurro", but as a Victor record it was backed by the "Macbeth" number, "Ah, la paterna mano". In Germany, as a double sided record it had "Spirito gentil" on the reverse side.

It is difficult to realize that this lovely example of early Italian operatic style was recorded at the same time as the previous record. This is the Caruso we all love. The high "C's" are taken effortlessly, and the legato is without blemish. Possibly the voice is already a shade darker than in the 1906 and 1907 records, but it is still incomparably lovely, and is used with the skill of a master of his craft. This record is most strongly recommended.

DON SEBASTIANO (Donizetti) **"In terra solo"**.

Heritage Series E.M. 38. Record 15-1037 A.

Apparently recorded at the same time as the record just reviewed— January 10th, 1908—but sung at such a break-neck speed that one wonders if it was ever meant to be anything more than a trial trip to determine the tempo at which the aria must be taken so as to be within the compass of a 12 inch disc. This record was issued on vinylite in America in 1948, as one of the Heritage Series, with the November, 1909 Huguenots aria "Bianca al par" on the reverse side.

As an example of Caruso's singing, this recording is inferior to the previous recording of the same aria, owing largely to the faster tempo. The phrasing is almost identical, however, and the singing does not appear to me unduly hurried, until the middle of the second verse. The production seems a little more laboured than in the first "take".

The following two records were made in New York on February 7th, 1908

LUCIA DI LAMMERMOOR (Donizetti) **"Chi mi frena"** (with Sembrich, Scotti, Journet, Severina and Daddi).

Matrix No. 5052. Victor S/S Cat. No. 96200. D/S Cat. No. 10001A. H.M.V. S/S Cat. No. 054205. D/S Cat. No. D.Q. 101. German Cat. No. 79003.

Issued in England in June, 1908, this record, the first of the three of this sextet in which Caruso took part, remained on the H.M.V. General Catalogue until 1946. As D.Q. 101, it was coupled with the

40

famous Rigoletto quartet made at the same time, and as a Victor double sided disc, it had the same coupling, and was available in U.S.A. from May, 1908 until 1924. On the Continent in double sided form it was backed by the Rigoletto Quartet in which Tetrazzini took part.

In the opening passages Caruso's voice is quite well recorded, and he sings magnificently. As a record, however, I find this rather unsatisfactory, as the primitive horn could not cope successfully with six voices at once, and the texture of the concerted passages is too muddy. The individual voices do not stand out, although Caruso is heard to good advantage in his short solo passages.

RIGOLETTO (Verdi) "**Bella figlia dell'amore**" (with Scotti, Sembrich & Severina).

> Matrix No. 5053. Victor S/S Cat. No. 96001. D/S Cat. No. 10001B. H.M.V. S/S Cat. No. 054199. D/S Cat. No. D.Q. 101. German Cat. No. 79001.

The English history of this record has been identical with that of the Lucia record just reviewed. Issued in England in 1908 (June) it was deleted from the H.M.V. General Catalogue in 1946. It was in 1924 that with almost every other Caruso recording, it became part of a double sided disc. In U.S.A. where it had the same coupling as in this country, it was available from April, 1908 until 1924. As a German disc it had as its companion record the "La Bohème" quartet.

Here the recording is more satisfactory than in the Lucia disc of the same date. Caruso's opening solo is superb, and alone makes the record desirable. Severina is excellent, and Sembrich sings easily, although her voice sounds lifeless. Again, as a version of the Rigoletto quartet, I could not recommend this, but as a souvenir of Caruso, it is most important.

The following records were all made in Camden in March, 1908

This is an important session, for nearly two years were to elapse before the next one, and during that time occurred the vocal breakdown which necessitated the cancellation of Caruso's engagements at the Metropolitan Opera House, and a return to Italy which culminated in the throat operation performed by Professor della Vedona, in Milan, during the spring of 1909. The authors think that while some of the

41

records made in this session, as for example the "Questa o quella" and the "Ah si ben mio", shows Caruso's powers still undiminished, others reveal the first traces of what was to become more evident in later years.

RIGOLETTO (Verdi) **"La donna è mobile"**. Recorded March 16th, 1908.

> Matrix No. 6033. Victor S/S Cat. No. 87017. D/S Cat. No. 500A. H.M.V. S/S Cat. No. 2-52641. D/S Cat. No. D.A. 561. German Cat. Nos. 74522 and 80007.

This, Caruso's third and final recording of the aria, was issued in England in June, 1908, and kept its place in the H.M.V. General Catalogue till the issue of the No. 2 (Historic records) in 1924, in which as D.A. 561, it was coupled with the aria from "Otello"—"Ora e per sempre addio". It was deleted in 1942. As a Victor double sided record it was coupled with the "Questa o quella" recorded at the same time, and was available in U.S.A. from June, 1908 until 1940. In Germany it had as its companion record, "Di quella pira" from "Il Trovatore".

In its original form, this record is perhaps the best of the three versions which Caruso left, for all round merit. It has the right atmosphere, and the singing is masterly. The cadenza at the close is superbly handled, with amazing agility, and the only criticism I can make is that the top "B" on the final note is a little forced in tone. I do not recommend the re-recorded version of this aria, with an electrically recorded accompaniment superimposed. The voice sounds harder than in the original.

RIGOLETTO (Verdi) **"Questa o quella"**. Recorded March 16th, 1908.

> Matrix No. 6035. Victor S/S Cat. No. 87018. D/S Cat. No. 500B. H.M.V. S/S Cat. No. 2-52642. D/S Cat. No. D.A. 102. German Cat. Nos. 74523 and 80009.

This is also Caruso's third and final recording of this aria. It was issued at the same time as the "La Donna" (June, 1908), but subsequently had a rather different history, remaining on the H.M.V. General Catalogue until 1946. As D.A. 102, it was coupled with the "Dì tu se fedele" from "Un Ballo in Maschera", but as a Victor double sided disc, it had as its companion the "La Donna" record just reviewed, and was in print from June, 1908 until 1940. As a German record, it had the same coupling as in England.

This is a supreme example of art concealing art. Caruso sings with the greatest possible abandon, yet the rhythm is perfect, and the high notes ring out with the greatest ease. The atmosphere has never been caught to anything like the same extent in any other recorded performance and the style of the whole aria, with its perfectly managed cadenza is the perfection of elegance. This is not a showy record, in the usual Italian manner, there are no overlong high notes, and no dramatic or musical excesses, yet to the connoisseur it shows unmistakable evidence of the complete technical mastery which Caruso possessed.

MADAMA BUTTERFLY (Puccini "**O quanti occhi fisi**". (with Farrar) Recorded March 10th, 1908.

> Matrix No. 6026. Victor S/S Cat. No. 89017. D/S Cat. No. 8011A. H.M.V. S/S Cat. No. 054201. D/S Cat. No. D.M. 110. German Cat. No. 78515.

Issued in England in June, 1908, this record remained in the H.M.V. General Catalogue until 1946. As D.M. 110 and as a Victor double sided disc, it was coupled with the letter duet from "Manon", as it was also in Germany. It was on general release in America from May, 1908 until 1928.

This is a most satisfactory record from both singer's points of view. Farrar's voice is pure and clear, and rises easily to the high "C" in the finale, and Caruso is at his most mellifluous. His phrase "E notte serena" is an example of the most beautiful cantabile singing, and the thrilling climax is never overdone. I have recently played this record immediately after the version by Sheridan and Pertile, and have never heard a clearer example of the difference between true expression obtained by legitimate means, as exemplified by Caruso and Farrar, and cheap sentimentality, so ably demonstrated by Pertile.

LA BOHEME (Puccini) "**Addio dolce svegliari**" (with Farrar, Scotti and Viafora). Recorded March 10th, 1908.

> Matrix No. 6025. Victor S/S Cat. No. 96002. D/S Cat. No. 10007A. H.M.V. S/S Cat. No. 054204. D/S Cat. No. D.O. 101. German Cat. Nos. 79002 and 79001.

Issued in this country in 1908, this record retained its place on the H.M.V. General Catalogue till 1946, when it perished in the general holocaust of Caruso's concerted numbers which that year witnessed. As D.O. 101 it was backed by the duet from "Mignon"—"Le duo des hirondelles", sung by Farrar and Journet, but as a Victor double sided disc it was coupled with the "La Bohème" duet "Mimi è ver" sung by Farrar and Scotti. It was on general release in America from May, 1908 until 1930. In Germany, as a double sided disc, it had the "Rigoletto quartet" in which Sembrich took part, on the reverse side.

Again this version sounds less lacrymose and consequently more moving than most of the subsequent ones. Caruso's singing of "Ch'io da vero poeta, rimavo con carezze" could hardly be bettered, and throughout his voice sounds easy, and the high "B" flats are beautifully lyrical. This is a most charming record.

IL TROVATORE (Verdi) **"Ah si ben mio coll' essere"**. Recorded March 16th, 1908.

> Matrix No. 6034. Victor S/S Cat. No. 88121. D/S Cat. No. 6002B. H.M.V. S/S Cat. No. 052210. D/S Cat. No. D.B. 112. German Cat. Nos. 76079 and 85019.

Issued in England in June, 1908, this record was transferred to the No. 2 Historic Catalogue in 1924, from which it was deleted in 1942, Its date of recording was given in the No. 2 List as 1907, but this is only one of a number of inaccuracies contained in that list —the 1906 "Di quella pira" for example is there dated 1910 and the matrix number of "Ah si ben mio" confirms the date assigned to it by the Victor Company in correspondence with the writer in 1933. As collectors may be surprised at the transferrence to the No. 2 List of such wonderful specimens of Caruso's singing as the "Un di', all'azzurro" and "Ah si ben mio", it may be worth noting here that the No. 2 List contained for many years some of the very greatest of all Caruso's records.

As a double sided disc, it was here coupled with "O tu che in seno agli angeli" from "La forza del destino" but in America, where it was in print from June, 1908 until 1933, it had the 1917 recording of "M'appari" from "Marta" as its companion. In Germany it had on the reverse side "Parmi veder le lagrime" from "Rigoletto".

This is superb singing of classical perfection, such as Caruso could do so beautifully. The legato is wonderfully maintained, the mood of quiet reflection is achieved by this simple expedient. There are no sobs, no distortions of rhythms, and no unnecessary dynamics, and yet the results are far more moving than some of the over exaggerated and sentimentalised versions of today. The quality of voice, and the legato do all that is necessary.

"Lolita" (Buzzi-Peccia). Recorded March 16th, 1908.

Matrix No. 6032. Victor S/S Cat. No. 88120. D/S Cat. No. 6003B. H.M.V. S/S Cat. No. 062005. D/S Cat. No. D.B. 696. German Cat. Nos. 76153 and 85042.

This record too, was issued in this country in June, 1908, was transferred to the No. 2 List in 1924, and finally disappeared in 1942. As D.B. 696, it was coupled with Caruso's final recording of "Cielo e mar" made in March 1910, but as a Victor double sided disc it had on the reverse side the 1906 "Che gelida manina". It was available in U.S.A. from 1908 until 1940. In 1951, "Lolita" was re-issued by H.M.V. as V.B. 60, in their Archive Series, with the November, 1911 "Eternamente" on the reverse side. The composer of "Lolita"—Buzzi —Peccia, was the subject of a very unflattering caricature by the great singer, to be found in the well-known volume of Caruso's caricatures published by Marzial Sisca, the editor of "La follia di New York".

As a German disc it had the same coupling as it was subsequently to have as an Archive record—"Eternamente".

I can find little to admire in this very ordinary song. Why Caruso chose to grace it with his voice is difficult to understand. It is like so many more pseudo Spanish songs of the period, complete with castanets, and yet so little like true Spanish music! Caruso sings it with great beauty, fluency and élan, but why?

IL TROVATORE (Verdi) **"Ai nostri monti"** (with Homer). Recorded March 17th, 1908.

Matrix No. 6036. Victor S/S Cat. No. 89018. H.M.V. S/S Cat. No. 054198.

This is the first of the three versions of this famous duet in which Caruso took part. Issued in England in June, 1908, it never avowedly lost its place in the H.M.V. General Catalogue until 1946. Actually, however, it was withdrawn in 1910, and replaced by the second version made in 1910, in which Homer again sang Azucena's music. This was done without any publicity, under the same matrix and catalogue numbers.

Our March, 1908 record is therefore something of a rarity, as it only had a selling history of about two years. The two records differ in a number of ways, the most noticeable of which is that in the earlier version Caruso ends an octave lower than in the 1910 re-recording, as he also does in the 1913 version in which Schumann Heink is his partner. The 1908 record of course never had an existence as a double sided disc, either here or in U.S.A., but the later one was both as an H.M.V. and Victor record, coupled with the "Mal reggendo" made in the same month—December, 1910—with Louise Homer. In America the 1908 rendering was in circulation from June, 1908 until 1911.

This first version, where Caruso takes the low note at the end, is also by far the best. The beautifully sung recitative which Caruso sings, beginning with the phrase "Riposa o madre" is one of the highlights of the duet, and fully demonstrates Caruso's amazing breath capacity. Homer's voice is not entirely satisfying as recorded. It sounds decidedly unsympathetic here.

AIDA (Verdi) **"Celeste Aida"**. Recorded March 29th, 1908.

Matrix No. 3180. First and only Victor Cat. No. 88127. H.M.V. S/S Cat. No. 052224. D/S Cat. No. D.B. 144. German Cat. Nos. 78512 and 85020.

This is the fourth of the five records of this title made by Caruso, and the first with orchestral accompaniment. The matrix number suggests a 1906 recording, but it is known that the first "take" which was recorded in 1906, was never issued, and the record we are now discussing was recorded on the date given above. Issued here in the summer of 1908, it survived the vicissitudes of the years and kept its place in the H.M.V. General catalogue until June, 1951. As D.B. 144, it was coupled with the September, 1919 recording of "Mia piccirella". It has apparently never had an existence as a double sided record in U.S.A., where it was only available from July, 1908 until 1912, when it was deleted and replaced by the issue of the version with recitative. In Germany as 78512 it had the Bohème" duet with Melba as its companion record, while as 85020 it was coupled with the "Addio alla madre" from "Cavalleria Rusticana".

This recording strikes a happy balance between the earlier and later recordings of the same aria. There is more intensity than in the 1904 recording, and at the same time the voice is still almost as beautiful as in the earlier records. The final "B" flat is most beautifully taken, though why the singer makes a crescendo on it, in view of Verdi's very definite instructions, is hard to say. He attacks it in a real mezza voce, but instead of making a diminuendo, he does the opposite. This is all in all, our favourite version of the aria.

The following eleven records were made in Camden in November, 1909

Though the latter part of this year saw Caruso's voice restored as the result of the removal of a node from one of his vocal chords, and owing partly also, no doubt, to a prolonged rest, it was now no longer quite the voice of 1905, 6 and 7. Having heard Caruso sing three months before this session, we can say with some confidence that the recording does him real justice and that the changes in voice and singing are faithfully reflected in these ten discs. A comparison of the two renderings of the Flower Song from "Carmen" which were made at this session, with the one made in February, 1905, and also of the two renderings of the "Huguenots" aria, will we think, afford ample proof of what we have written. However, all these records, and the "Ah che la morte ognora" from "Il Trovatore" are very fine indeed and were not to be surpassed in the coming years.

Owing no doubt to his long absence from the recording studios, there was great anxiety to put these November, 1909 records on the market as soon as possible. Not only were they made available to the American public in the next month, but so eager were His Master's Voice to break the silence that they were issued in this country almost at the same time. The writer sees from his diary that he received his copy of "Magiche Note" on Thursday, December 16th—less than six weeks after Caruso had recorded it in New York, and in an issue of the "Gramophone News" appearing about this time, and which is before him as he writes, a whole page H.M.V. advertisement is devoted to four records made at this session, of which "Magiche Note" is one. The other three were "Mamma mia che vo' sapé?", "Pour un baiser", and "O tu che in seno agli angeli". The heading was "Caruso—latest Gramophone Records".

LA FORZA DEL DESTINO (Verdi) **"O tu che in seno agli angeli".** Recorded November 6th, 1909.

Matrix No. 8345. Victor S/S Cat. No. 88207. D/S Cat. No. 6000B. H.M.V. S/S Cat. No. 2-052006. D/S Cat. No. D.B. 112. German Cat. Nos. 76091 and 85022.

Issued in England about two months after its recording, this record was transferred to the No. 2 List in 1924, and was finally deleted in

1942. As D.B. 112 it was backed by "Ah, si ben mio" from "Il Trovatore", but as a Victor double sided record it had the 1911 rendering of "Celeste Aida" on the reverse side. Although exactly nine years were to elapse before Caruso's first appearance in this opera, the record, and the duets with Scotti and Amato made in 1906 and 1911, are evidence of the singer's early interest in "La Forza del Destino", which as yet he presumably judged to be too heavy for his voice. This record was available in the U.S.A. from December, 1909 until 1952. In Germany it had as a double sided record the final recording of "Celeste Aida" as its companion.

The opening recitative is superbly sung, and is a magnificent example of declamation combined with bel canto. The aria could have been opened more quietly, and then the contrast with the recitative would have been even more effective. As it is, it is a magnificent example of Caruso's singing in 1909.

"Mamma mia che vo'sapè (Nutile). Recorded November 6th, 1909.

> Matrix No. 8344. Victor S/S Cat. No. 88206. D/S Cat. No. 6009B. H.M.V. S/S Cat. No. 2-052005. D/S Cat. No. D.B. 119. German Cat. Nos. 76090 and 85021.

This record was issued in England about three months after its recording, and retained its place on the H.M.V. General Catalogue until 1941. As D.B. 119 it was coupled with "Pe'chè?", but as a Victor double sided disc it had "I' m'arricordo e Napule" on the reverse side. In Germany it was coupled with "Manella Mia". It was available in U.S.A. from December, 1909 until 1933.

I suppose this is well sung, in the usual Caruso manner, but once again I fail to see the necessity of this recording. When one thinks of the operatic work which Caruso might have recorded in its place, it all seems rather futile. The voice in the finale seems a little pushed.

TOSCA (Puccini) **"E lucevan le stelle".** Recorded November 6th, 1909.

> Matrix No. 8346. Victor S/S Cat. No. 87044. D/S Cat. No. 511A. H.M.V. S/S Cat. No. 7-52002. D/S Cat. No. D.A. 112. German Cat. Nos. 74526 and 80010.

This Caruso's fifth and final essay at this title was issued here in August, 1910 and at the time of writing—August, 1955—it still retains its place in the H.M.V. General Catalogue, (being one of the few discs still to survive). In its double sided form, both as an H.M.V. and

48

Victor record it was backed by the "Recondita Armonia" recorded on the same day, and in Germany it had the same coupling. It was available in U.S.A. from December, 1909 until 1940.

This is undoubtedly Caruso's finest version of the famous aria, for all round merit. The vocal tone is not quite so beautiful as in the 1904 version, but the authority of it all, the easy resonance, and the drama without undue melodramatic effects all combine to make it outstanding.

TOSCA (Puccini) **"Recondita Armonia"**. Recorded November 6th, 1909.

> Matrix No. 8347. Victor S/S Cat. No. 87043. D/S Cat. No. 511B. H.M.V. S/S Cat. No. 7-52004. D/S Cat. No. D.A. 112. German Cat. Nos. 74528 and 80010.

The English history of this disc is exactly the same as that of the "E lucevan le stelle" just reviewed. The same remarks also apply to its history in U.S.A. and Germany.

This is one of Caruso's finest recordings of the period. The lyrical outburst is most beautifully managed, and never overdone, and the climax is thrilling in its sincerity and intensity.

"Pour un baiser" (Tosti). Recorded November 6th, 1909.

> Matrix No. 8343. Victor S/S Cat. No. 87042. D/S Cat. No. 517B. H.M.V. S/S Cat. No. 7-32000. D/S Cat. No. D.A. 118. Archive Series Cat. No. V.A. 35. German Cat. Nos. 74502 and 80002.

Issued in England in February, 1910, this record remained on the General H.M.V. Catalogue till 1924, when it was transferred to the No. 2 List, where it remained till 1941. As D.A. 118, it was backed by Tosti's "Parted", but as a Victor Double sided disc it had Tchaikowsky's "Pourquoi" on the reverse side, and in their Archive Series issue of this record, H.M.V. adopted in 1951 the Victor coupling. Those who heard Caruso sing "Pour un baiser" will perhaps recall how he lowered his head while singing the "dans un" at the close, and then raised it for the final "baiser". It was on sale as a Victor record from December, 1909 until 1927. In Germany it was coupled with Guy d'Hardelot's "Because".

I must confess to a liking for this quite ordinary little song, which is sung and phrased quite beautifully by Caruso, in that mood of quiet melancholy which suited him so perfectly.

AIDA (Verdi) **"O terra addio"** (with Gadski). Recorded November 6th, 1909.

> Matrix No. 8348. Victor S/S Cat. No. 89029. D/S Cat. No. 8015B. H.M.V. S/S Cat. No. 2-054006. D/S Cat. No. D.M. 114. German Cat. Nos. 78517 and 78516.

AIDA (Verdi) **"La fatal pietra"** (with Gadski). Recorded November 7th, 1909.

> Matrix No. 8353. Victor S/S Cat. No. 89028. D/S Cat. No. 8015A. H.M.V. S/S Cat. No. 2-054005. D/S Cat. No. D.M. 114. German Cat. No. 78516.

These two records were issued in England in July, 1910, and remained as single sided discs on the H.M.V. General Catalogue until 1923, when together they made the two sides of D.M. 114, and they only disappeared from the H.M.V. General Catalogue in 1946 with the rest of Caruso's concerted numbers. Both in U.S.A. and in Germany they were similarly coupled. In U.S.A. these records were on general release from January 1910 until 1930.

This is some of Caruso's finest singing of the period. On the first side the little solo commencing "Morir si pura e bella" is wonderfully sung, and the controlled high notes on the second side are most beautiful in quality, and demonstrate the perfection of Caruso's technique. Gadski is a worthy partner, and the concerted singing is of a very high order.

CARMEN (Bizet) **"Il fior che avevi a me tu dato"**. Recorded November 7th, 1909.

> Matrix No. 8349. Victor S/S Cat. No. 88209. D/S Cat. No. 6007B. H.M.V. S/S Cat. No. 2-052007. D/S Cat. No. D.B. 117. German Cat. Nos. 76092 and 85015.

Though recorded at the same time as the French version, this record for some reason was not issued in this country until September, 1911. However, having arrived it kept its place on the H.M.V. General Catalogue until the summer of 1950. As a double sided record, both here, in the U.S.A. and in Germany it was coupled with "O Paradiso". It was in general circulation in U.S.A. from December, 1909 until 1930.

There is no doubt that in many ways this is Caruso's finest recording of the Flower Song, and yet it has become too sophisticated, despite its obvious assuredness, to completely satisfy at least one listener. The voice too, has lost the velvet which is obvious in the earlier records. It is still the most beautiful of tenor voices, but a something, a golden glow, has gone, never to return.

CARMEN (Bizet) **"La fleur que tu m' avais jetée".** Recorded November 7th, 1909.

> Matrix No. 8350. Victor S/S Cat. No. 88208. D/S Cat. No. 6004A. H.M.V. S/S Cat. No. 2-032000. D/S Cat. No. D.B. 130. German Cat. Nos. 76015 and 85006.

This record was on the English market about five months after its recording in New York, and remained in the H.M.V. General Catalogue till the issue of the No. 2 List in 1924, when as D.B. 130 it was coupled with the "Ah fuyez douce image" from Massenet's "Manon", and was not deleted until 1942. As a Victor double sided record it was coupled with the 1906 "Salut! demeure" and was on general release from December, 1909 until 1933. As a German double sided record it was coupled with the 1903 "Pearl Fishers", "Mi par d'udir".

This, like the previous record, has many good points. The high notes have not quite the resonance of the Italian version, but there is possibly a finer portrayal of the character of the unhappy Don José. The difficult phrase, "Et j'étais une chose à toi", rising to the high "B" flat, is sung in one breath, and is rather hurried, suggesting that Caruso never quite overcame his early difficulty with this phrase. The French is not at all bad, despite typically Italian "R's", and a tendency to open the acute "E" sounds.

LES HUGUENOTS (Meyerbeer) **"Bianca al par di neve alpina".** Recorded November 7th, 1909.

> Matrix No. 8351. Victor S/S Cat. No. 88210. D/S Cat. No. 6005B. H.M.V. S/S Cat. No. 2-052008. D/S Cat. No. D.B. 115. Heritage Series Cat. No. E.M. 38. Record 15-1037B. German Cat. Nos. 76093 and 85011.

Issued in England soon after its recording, this record remained on the H.M.V. General Catalogue till its deletion in 1941. As D.B. 115 it was backed by the Crescenzo song "Uocchi celesti". In U.S.A. as 6005, it was coupled with the 1906 "Spirito gentil" and in the more recently issued "Heritage" series with the unissued version of the Don Sebastiano "In terra solo". As a German double sided disc it was coupled with the 1906 recorded Romance from "Marta". It was available in the U.S.A. from December, 1909 until 1933.

51

This record is beautifully sung, and the pealing high notes ring out with great effect. It is only in comparison with the effortless ease of the 1905 recording, that this example suffers slightly. The voice is bigger, and undoubtedly more dramatic, but it no longer flows quite as it had done four years previously. Nevertheless this is in every way a worthy example of Caruso's art, at this stage of his career.

REGINA DI SABA (Goldmark) **"Magiche Note"**. Recorded November 7th, 1909.

Matrix No. 6062. Victor S/S Cat. No. 87041. D/S Cat. No. 520A. H.M.V. S/S Cat. No. 7-52003. D/S Cat. No. D.A. 122. German Cat. Nos. 74527 and 80011. Archive Series Cat. No. V.A. 36.

For many years this was thought to be a March 1908 recording. The Victor Company gave this date to the present writer in 1933, when he was compiling the discography which appeared in the January, 1934 issue of "The Gramophone", and this mistake was repeated in later discographies including that also done by the writer for "Enrico Caruso, his life and death" by Dorothy Caruso, which appeared in 1946. This date was, however, corrected in the H.M.V. brochure containing the Archive Series Records, in October 1951. The origin of this mistake is to be found in the fact that Caruso did record this aria on March 29th, 1908, but apparently this "take" was never used. When, however, it was recorded by Caruso in November 1909, it had the same matrix number as had been assigned to it twenty months earlier —except for the substitution of "B" for "C", and this is probably responsible for the misdating of it by the Victor Company. The two far more widely separated recordings of "M'appari" made by Caruso, also had the same matrix numbers, only distinguished by the "1" and "2" following them. In this case however, the catalogue numbers did not follow the same course for H.M.V. never issued the 1917 "Marta" recording, except as an electrically re-created record, and Victor never issued the 1906 recording in double sided form. "Magiche Note" was issued in this country in December, 1909 and remained on the H.M.V. General Catalogue until its deletion in 1941. As a double sided disc it had Landon Ronald's "Sérénade Espagnole" as its companion record. As a Victor record it was available from December, 1909 until 1927, with the same coupling as in this country. In Germany it had the final recording of the "Siciliana" from "Cavalleria Rusticana" on the reverse side.

This is a most interesting record, for Caruso uses a curious covered tone almost throughout. The effect is to add a touch of mystery to the interpretation, and this quality, combined with some beautifully contrived climaxes, makes the record well worth while. The ending in a quaint mixture of mezza voce and falsetto, is not satisfactory, as recorded. Possibly it was more effective in the opera house. (In fairness, it must be stated that many people disagree with the writer's opinion of the concluding phrases, which have been described by authoritative critics as "delicious" and "truly magical"!).

Recorded January 6th, 1910. New York

IL TROVATORE (Verdi) **"Ah, che la morte ognora"** (with Alda and chorus).

> Matrix No. 8506. Victor S/S Cat. No. 89030. D/S Cat. No. 8042A. H.M.V. S/S Cat. No. 2-054007. D/S Cat. No. D.K. 119. German Cat. No. 78518.

Apparently several "takes" were made about the same time, of this title and it now seems certain that the "take" from which this version was pressed was not recorded, as had been thought previously, in December, 1909, but a few days later, in the following month. It was issued in July 1910 in England, and remained on the H.M.V. General Catalogue till 1928, when it was transferred to the No. 2 List, where it remained until its deletion in 1946. In its double sided form, it was backed, both as an H.M.V. and a Victor disc, by the January, 1913 "Ai nostri monti". In America this record was available from February, 1910 until 1953.

Alda's voice, as recorded, does not always accord with her great reputation. Here it is decidedly hard, but as a memento of Caruso in one of his most famous roles, it is very welcome. He sings well, and the smoothness of his vocal line, and the ease of his high notes are everywhere apparent.

(The Faust Garden scene records, which are reviewed next, were not all recorded on the same date. However, it would be senseless to review each record separately, although individual recordings, dates, matrix numbers etc., will be found under each title. The musical criticism will be found at the end).

The following seven "Faust" records were made in New York on January 6th, 12th and 17th, 1910

FAUST (Gounod) **"Seigneur Dieu"** (with Farrar, Gilibert and Journet). Recorded January 12th, 1910.

> Matrix No. 8544. Victor S/S Cat. No. 95204. D/S Cat. No. 10004A. H.M.V. S/S Cat. No. 2-034003. D/S Cat. No. D.M. 102. German Cat. No. 78500.

Issued in England in October, 1910, it remained on the H.M.V. General Catalogue until 1946. Both as an H.M.V. and Victor record, it was coupled, in double sided form, with the quartet "Eh quoi, toujours seule?". It was listed as a Victor record from May, 1910 until 1927.

FAUST (Gounod) **"Eh quoi, toujours seule?"** (with Farrar, Gilibert and Journet). Recorded January 12th, 1910.

> Matrix No. 8547. Victor S/S Cat. No. 95205. D/S Cat. No. 10004B. H.M.V. S/S Cat. No. 2-034004. D/S Cat. No. D.M. 102.

Issued in England in October, 1910, it remained on the H.M.V. General Catalogue until 1946. Both as an H.M.V. and Victor record it was issued in double sided form coupled with the quartet "Seigneur Dieu". It was on general release in the U.S.A. from May, 1910 until 1927.

FAUST (Gounod) **"Il se fait tard"** (with Farrar). Recorded January 6th, 1910.

> Matrix No. 8533. Victor S/S Cat. No. 89031. D/S Cat. No. 8009B. H.M.V. S/S Cat. No. 2-034011. D/S Cat. No. D.M. 108. German Cat. No. 78502.

Issued in England in October, 1910, it remained on the H.M.V. General Catalogue until 1946. Both as an H.M.V., a Victor, and a German double sided disc, it was coupled with "O nuit d'amour". It was available in U.S.A. from May, 1910 until 1928.

FAUST (Gounod) **"O Nuit d'amour"** (with Farrar). Recorded January 6th, 1910.

> Matrix No. 8534. Victor S/S Cat. No. 89032. D/S Cat. No. 8009A. H.M.V. S/S Cat. No. 2-034012. D/S Cat. No. D.M. 108. German Cat. Nos. 78502 and 78503.

Issued in England in October, 1910, this record remained on the H.M.V. General Catalogue until 1946. Both as an H.M.V. and Victor double sided disc, it was coupled with the record last reviewed, as it also was in Germany. It was on the Victor Catalogue from May, 1910 until 1928.

FAUST (Gounod) **"Elle ouvre sa fenêtre"** (with Farrar and Journet). Recorded January 17th, 1910.

Matrix No. 8558. Victor S/S Cat. No. 89040. D/S Cat. No. 10008B. H.M.V. S/S Cat. No. 2-034007. D/S Cat. No. D.K. 106.

Issued in England in October, 1910, this record remained on the H.M.V. General Catalogue until 1946. In England as a double sided disc, it was coupled with "Alerte, ou vous êtes perdus", but in U.S.A. it had this coupling but also as 8022 it was backed by the Mignon "Duo des hirondelles" sung by Farrar and Journet. It was available in U.S.A. from May, 1910 until 1933.

The five discs listed above, give a very fair covering of all the music from the beginning of the "Garden Scene" to the end of the act, with the exception of Mefistofele's solo "Il était temps". In fact this was the most nearly "complete" operatic series in which Caruso appeared. It was an innovation as far as Caruso recordings go, in that it gives us an opportunity of hearing the great tenor in more than just isolated snippets. Unfortunately the recording is rather tight, and less forward than in 1906-8, and the results, though smooth, are a trifle lacking in dynamics. Caruso sounds much more at home than in his earlier recordings in the French language, Farrar and Gilibert are both excellent, and Journet gives a notable interpretation of the part of Mephistopheles. The duet, following the "Garden Scene" proper, is exquisitely sung by both artists, and Caruso's mezza voce in the opening phrases "Eternelle, o nuit d'amour" is ravishingly beautiful. The record "Elle ouvre sa fenêtre" is included as a Caruso recording, since the great tenor's voice is heard on the disc, but as he only sings one word, collectors are warned that if they are expecting to hear more of Caruso, they may find this record an extravagance.

FAUST (Gounod) **"Mon coeur est pénétré"** (with Farrar). Recorded January 12th, 1910.

Matrix No. 8542. Victor S/S Cat. No. 89033. D/S Cat. No. 8010B. H.M.V. S/S Cat. No. 2-034005. D/S Cat. No. D.M. 109. German Cat. No. 78535.

Issued in England in 1910 (October), this disc remained on the H.M.V. General Catalogue until 1946. As an H.M.V., Victor, and

German double sided disc, it was coupled with "Attends, voici la rue".
It was available in U.S.A. from March, 1910 until 1927.

(For review see under the following title.)

FAUST (Gounod) **"Attends, voici la rue"** (with Farrar). Recorded
January 12th, 1910.

> Matrix No. 8543. Victor S/S Cat. No. 89034. D/S Cat. No. 8010A.
> H.M.V. S/S Cat. No. 2-034006. D/S Cat. No. D.M. 109. German Cat.
> Nos. 78536 and 78535.

Issued in England in October, 1910, this record remained on the
H.M.V. General Catalogue until 1946. Both as the H.M.V. and
Victor double sided disc, it was coupled with "Mon coeur est
pénétré" as it was in Germany. It remained on the Victor Catalogue
from March, 1910 until 1927.

These two sides contain some excellent singing from both Caruso
and Farrar, the latter in particular singing most beautifully in the
second part. These two sides, together with the duets following the
Garden Scene proper, are possibly the best of the Faust excerpts.

Recorded January 12th, 1910. New York

MARTA (Flotow) **"Solo profugo"** (with Journet).

> Matrix No. 8546. Victor S/S Cat. No. 89036. D/S Cat. No. 8016B. H.M.V.
> S/S Cat. No. 2-054010. D/S Cat. No. D.M. 115. German Cat. No. 78519.

This record was issued in England in August, 1910, and remained
on the H.M.V. General Catalogue until 1946. It was backed, as a
double sided record by the Faust duet "O merveille" in England,
U.S.A. and Germany. As a Victor record it was available from March,
1910 until 1927.

Caruso's singing of the opening solo is one of his finest achievements
among the 1910 recordings. The high notes are beautifully poised,
and there is a lovely lyrical quality throughout. He is well partnered
by Journet, and in the concerted passages the two voices blend admirably. There are some fine crescendos on the two high "B" flats,
which are taken softly, and then expanded without any hardening of
the tone.

56

The following three "Faust" records were made in New York on January 16th, 1910

FAUST (Gounod) "O, merveille" (with Journet).

Matrix No. 8555. Victor S/S Cat. No. 89039. D/S Cat. No. 8016A. H.M.V. S/S Cat. No. 2-034000. D/S Cat. No. D.M. 115 German Cat. Nos. 78537 and 78519.

Issued in England in October, 1910, it remained with the other Caruso Faust records on the H.M.V. General Catalogue till 1946. In 1923 it was coupled with "Solo profugo" from Marta, as it was in U.S.A. and Germany. It was available in U.S.A. from April, 1910 until 1927.

This disc contains some typical singing on the part of both artists and yet it is disappointing when one considers what it might have been! It is lacking in dynamics, and the recording is safe but unexciting.

FAUST (Gounod) **"Que voulez-vous messieurs?"** (with Scotti & Journet).

Matrix No. 8556. Victor S/S Cat. No. 95206. D/S Cat. No. 10011A. H.M.V. S/S Cat. No. 2-034001. D/S Cat. No. D.O. 100. German Cat. No. 78539.

Issued in England in 1910 and remaining on the H.M.V. General Catalogue until 1946, it was backed when it became a double sided disc after 1924, by the February, 1907 "Rigoletto" Quartet, it was available from June, 1910 until 1924. In Germany, as a double sided disc, it was coupled with the Lombardi Trio, "Qual volutta trascorrere".

Again this recording cannot be wholeheartedly recommended. The tenor's voice only succeeds in sounding more than adequate on one or two high notes. Scotti sounds rather tight and throaty, and certainly not at his best, and Journet has little opportunity.

FAUST (Gounod) **"Alerte! ou vous êtes perdus"** (with Farrar & Journet).

Matrix No. 8545. Victor S/S Cat. No. 95203. D/S Cat. No. 10008A. H.M.V. S/S Cat. No. 2-034002. D/S Cat. No. D.K. 106. German Cat. No. 78538.

Issued in England in October, 1910, it remained on the H.M.V. General Catalogue until 1946. In this country its only coupling has been with the trio "Elle ouvre sa fenêtre", but in U.S.A. it was coupled not only with this, but alternatively with the February, 1919 trio from "Samson and Delilah", and was available from March, 1910 until 1933.

This is a most disappointing record from the point of view of the collector of Caruso records, since he is quite overpowered by the other singers. This is probably due to their respective positions in relation to the recording horn, but whatever the cause, it makes a poor record, from the point of view of balance. Farrar is, however, magnificent.

The following five records were made in New York on March 14th, 1910

LA GIOCONDA (Ponchielli) "Cielo e mar!"

Matrix No. 8718. Victor S/S Cat. No. 88246. D/S Cat. No. 6020A. H.M.V. S/S Cat. No. 2-052032. D/S Cat. No. D.B. 696. German Cat. Nos. 76094 and 85016.

Issued in England in February, 1911, this third and final "Cielo e mar" remained on the General Catalogue until the appearance of the No. 2 List, in November, 1924, to which it was then transferred, and where it remained till 1942. As a double sided H.M.V. disc, it was backed by the March, 1908 "Lolita", but as a Victor record it had the aria "Ah fuyez douce image" from Massenet's "Manon" on the reverse side, and was available in U.S.A. from September, 1910 until 1930. In Germany it had the "Andrea Chénier" aria "Un di all' azzurro" as its companion record.

There is little to choose between this version, and the 1905 one, for all round excellence. Both have their points, and although the earlier recording shows us a more lyrical note, and an easier approach to the high notes, these qualities are compensated for in the above disc, by much better recording, a triumphant ring at the climaxes, and an orchestral accompaniment which is certainly preferable to the piano in such music. Both versions are highly commended.

GERMANIA (Franchetti) "No non chiuder gli occhi vaghi".

Matrix No. 8713. Victor S/S Cat. No. 87054. D/S Cat. No. 508A. H.M.V. S/S Cat. No. 7-52014. D/S Cat. No. D.A. 543. German Cat. Nos. 74559 and 80022.

Issued in England in September, 1910, this third and final recording of this aria was transferred to the No. 2 List in 1924, and was finally deleted in 1942. Both as an H.M.V. and Victor double sided disc this title was backed by the "Studenti udite" aria made at the same time as it also was as a German issue. These two recordings were reissued by H.M.V. in 1951 in their Archive series as V.A. 38. In U.S.A. this record was available from 1910 until 1924.

Although this aria is beautifully sung, and is more lyrical than most of his interpretations of this period, it lacks the delicacy of the earlier renderings of March, 1902. To compensate for this, the climaxes are made more of, there is an orchestra of sorts, in place of the piano, and the record is much easier to find than either of the two 1902 versions.

GERMANIA (Franchetti) "**Studenti udite**".

> Matrix No. 8710. Victor S/S Cat. No. 87053. D/S Cat. No. 508B. H.M.V. S/S Cat. No. 7-52013. D/S Cat. No. D.A. 543. German Cat. Nos. 74558 and 80022.

Issued in England in September, 1910, this second and final rendering of this title was transferred to the No. 2 List in 1924, and was deleted in 1942. Here, in U.S.A. and in Germany it was coupled with the "No non chiuder" aria, and re-appeared with that title to make both sides of the Archive issue V.A. 38. It was on general release in U.S.A. from June, 1910 until 1924.

Little need be added to the remarks on the previous record. Compared with the earlier one, it has the advantage of better recording, greater dynamics, and the orchestra. Against this, is the fact that the voice is no longer quite so beautiful as in the very first recordings.

MADAMA BUTTERFLY (Puccini) "**Amore o grillo**" (with Scotti).

> Matrix No. 8711. Victor S/S Cat. No. 89043. D/S Cat. No. 8014B. H.M.V. S/S Cat. No. 2-054014. D/S Cat. No. D.M. 113. German Cat. Nos. 78521 and 78520.

This record was issued in England shortly after its recording. It was in the "Celebrity" section of the H.M.V. General Catalogue from February to July, 1911, and remained on it till its deletion in 1946. Both as an H.M.V. double 'sided disc after 1923, and as one side of 8014B in U.S.A., this title was backed by the "Non ve l'avevo detto" duet made at the same time with Scotti, and as a German issue it also had this backing. It was on general release in America from July 1910 until 1928.

It is perhaps surprising to find that Caruso lent his voice to such an ungrateful character as Pinkerton. After the first act he has little to do, but that first act does contain some fine moments for the tenor, and Caruso sang Puccini to perfection. In this duet, his high notes ring out with great splendour, and his phrasing is a joy. Scotti is equally at home in one of his most famous roles. Caruso's pronunciation of the word "whiskey" is most amusing.

MADAMA BUTTERFLY (Puccini) **"Non ve l'avevo detto"** (with Scotti).

> Matrix No. 8712. Victor S/S Cat. No. 89047. D/S Cat. No. 8014A. H.M.V. S/S Cat. No. 2-054013. D/S Cat. No. D.M. 113. German Cat. No. 78520.

This record, with the one last reviewed, was in the "Celebrity" section of the H.M.V. General Catalogue for February to July, 1911, and remained on it till its deletion in 1946. Both here and in America and Germany, as a double sided record after 1923, it was coupled with the "Amore o grillo" duet with Scotti, made at the same time. It was on the Victor Catalogue from August, 1910 until 1928.

Again Caruso takes full advantage of all his opportunities, and his voice is a constant joy. His farewell to the "fiorito asil" is most poignant, and never overdone. It is in fact an object lesson to the many super lacrymose tenors who now adorn the stage in Italy.

The following four records were made in Camden on December 28th, 1910

"For you alone" (Geehl).

> Matrix No. 9744. Victor S/S Cat. No. 87070. D/S Cat. Nos. 507 and 1658. H.M.V. S/S Cat. No. 4-2122. D/S Cat. No. D.A. 108. German Cat. No. 80000.

Caruso's first recording in English was issued in England in April, 1911. It kept its place on the H.M.V. General List until 1950. Both as an H.M.V. and a Victor record it was coupled with his final recording in English "A Dream", but in Germany it was backed by "Love is mine". The record was on general release in U.S.A. from February, 1911 until 1933.

This, the first of Caruso's recordings in English, is in some ways the best. The song which is of little consequence, is well written for the great tenor's voice, and works up to a climax at the end, in such a way that it is most singable. The high notes are resonant and clear, and the pronunciation of English is quite charming in its way, and not a little amusing in places.

OTELLO (Verdi) **"Ora e per sempre addio sante memorie".**

> Matrix No. 9743. Victor S/S Cat. No. 87071. D/S Cat. No. 505B. H.M.V. S/S Cat. No. 7-52017. D/S Cat. No. D.A. 561. German Cat. Nos. 74529 and 80013.

This record was issued in England in April, 1911, and remained on the H.M.V. General Catalogue as long as it was in single sided form. In 1924 it took its place in double sided form in the No. 2 List from which it was not deleted until 1942. In this country it was backed by the March, 1908 "La donna è mobile" and as a Victor and German record by the Manon Lescaut aria "Donna non vidi mai". It remained on the Victor Catalogue from February, 1911 until 1930.

I find this a disappointing record. Caruso was known to have studied Otello, but he continually put off any appearance in this role, awaiting further development of his dramatic powers. In this recording the voice sounds pinched, and at times a little strained. There is a certain striving after effect. It may be the recording, which is not very good, but one thing is quite certain—it is not really representative of the greatest tenor of his generation. There are better versions by Tamagno and Zenatello.

N.B. Since reviewing the above record, I have heard a transfer on an extended play record, Victor ERAT I, and have formed a much more favourable opinion of the disc.

I PAGLIACCI (Leoncavallo) **"No Pagliaccio non son!"**

> Matrix No. 9742. Victor S/S Cat. No. 88279. D/S Cat. No. 6001A. H.M.V. S/S Cat. No. 2-052034. H.M.V. D/S Cat. No. D.B. 111. German Cat. Nos. 76095 and 85017.

Issued in England in April, 1911, it is one of the very few original Caruso records, (we do not count the electrically revivified issues as such) still to keep its place in the H.M.V. General Catalogue. Both here and in U.S.A. and in Germany, in its double sided form it has been coupled with the 1907 "Vesti la giubba". It was available in U.S.A. from 1911 until 1953.

Although Caruso recorded "Vesti la giubba" on three different occasions, this is the only known version of Canio's later outburst which he has left us. It is in every way very fine. There is full realisation of the drama of the scene, the voice rises magnificently to the full demands of the climaxes, and the central lyrical portion is a choice example of the best Caruso cantilena. This is a superb example of Caruso's art at this period of his life.

CAVALLERIA RUSTICANA (Mascagni) "Siciliana".

Matrix No. 9745. Victor S/S Cat. No. 87072. D/S Cat. No. 516B. H.M.V. S/S Cat. No. 7-52018. D/S Cat. No. D.A. 117. German Cat. Nos. 74530 and 80011.

Issued in England in 1911, this, the fourth and final recording of this aria retained its place on the H.M.V. General Catalogue until 1946. Greatly admired by the late Hermann Klein it was broadcast by him shortly before his death. Both in this country and in U.S.A. it was, as a double sided disc backed by the Andrea Chenier aria "Come un bel di di Maggio". In U.S.A. it was on general release from 1911 until 1933. In Germany its companion record was Goldmark's Queen of Sheba aria "Magiche note".

This famous recording is one of the very best Caruso has left us, considering all things. To begin with, it is a first rate acoustic recording, and the harp accompaniment loses far less than an orchestra does by this process. Caruso's singing is very fine in every way, and the management of the voice in the mezza voce final phrases, is excellent.

The following five records were made in Camden on December 29th, 1910

"Addio" (Tosti).

Matrix No. 9747. Victor S/S Cat. No. 88280. D/S Cat. Nos. 6021A and 7156. H.M.V. S/S Cat. Nos. 2-052035 and 42-754. D/S Cat. Nos. D.B. 131 and D.B. 1386. German Cat. Nos. 76096 and 85027.

Issued in this country in April, 1911, it was deleted in 1941. It was first coupled as a double sided disc both in this country and in U.S.A. with the April, 1917 "Musica proibita" and later both countries issued it with the September, 1920 "Africana" title "Deh! ch'io ritorni". It was on the Victor list from February, 1911 until 1933. As a German double sided record it was coupled with "Cujus animam" (Stabat Mater).

The voice sounds a little hard on this disc, although the legato is as perfect as ever. The ending which owes nothing to the composer, is not an entire success, and in fact shows signs of strain. On the whole this record is not a great success, and it is maddening to think what might have been done in its place!

IL TROVATORE (Verdi) **"Ai nostri monti"** (with Homer).

> Matrix No. 6036. Victor S/S Cat. No. 89018. D/S Cat. No. 8013A. H.M.V. S/S Cat. No. 054198. D/S Cat. No. D.M. 112. German Cat. No. 78514.

Some ambiguity necessarily attaches to the history of this, Caruso's second recording of this famous duet, for it was silently substituted in the catalogues for its March, 1908 predecessor under the same matrix and catalogue numbers. It is impossible to differentiate between the two versions by any catalogue description. One attempt to do so by giving the two matrix numbers CA 6036 and C.A. 6036 is of no value for many copies of this 1910 version—even in double sided form— only have on them A. 6036, as the copies of the 1908 recording did. But the most casual hearing of the two versions at once reveals the very considerable differences between them, the most noticeable of which is the ending by Caruso in the 1910 recording, an octave higher than he did in 1908. Our 1910 record was no doubt made available as soon as possible after its recording, and then remained on the H.M.V. General Catalogue until 1946. In its double sided form here after 1923, and as a U.S.A. and German issue, it was coupled with the "Mal reggendo" duet made with Louise Homer at this same session. It remained on the Victor list from 1911 until 1928.

This replacement, although a better recording from the engineers' point of view, is much less attractive from the tenor's. His voice has hardened and darkened in the course of the two years, and the superb easy flow of the earlier version and the almost miraculous breathing are replaced by what is a more dramatic reading, but a much less desirable one in many ways.

IL TROVATORE (Verdi) **"Mal reggendo"** (with Homer).

> Matrix No. 6682. Victor S/S Cat. No. 89049. D/S Cat. No. 8013B. H.M.V. S/S Cat. No. 2-054017. D/S Cat. No. D.M. 112. German Cat. Nos. 78524 and 78514.

Issued in England in September, 1911, this record kept its place on the H.M.V. General Catalogue until 1946. Both here, in U.S.A. and in Germany, it was coupled with the "Ai nostri monti" made at the same session. It remained on general release as a Victor record from March, 1911 until 1928. It is interesting to note that Caruso and Homer had previously made a recording of this duet in December, 1908, but this was never issued.

Although this lacks the lyrical touches of the first recording of "Ai nostri monti" it is nevertheless very fine in every way, and after all, lyrical qualities would be almost out of place in this impassioned duet, in which Homer joins quite admirably. It is in every way authoritative, and quite representative of Caruso's art.

AIDA (Verdi) **"Già i sacerdoti adunansi"** (with Homer).

> Matrix No. 9748. Victor S/S Cat. No. 89050. D/S Cat. No. 8012B. II.M.V. S/S Cat. No. 2-054015. D/S Cat. No. D.K. 115. German Cat. No. 78522.

This record took nearly ten years to find its way to this country, not being issued here until May, 1920. It was transferred to the No. 2 List after 1923 as D.K. 115, where it was coupled with the December, 1911 "Celeste Aida", being deleted in 1946. As a Victor double sided disc, it was backed, as one would expect it would have been in England, by the "Aida a me togliesti" duet with Homer, made at the same session, and was recently re-issued with the same backing in the Heritage Series as 15-1025. It was on general release as a Victor record from March, 1911 until 1928. In Germany as a double sided record it had the same backing as in the U.S.A.

(For review, see the succeeding record).

AIDA (Verdi) **"Aida a me togliesti"** (with Homer).

> Matrix No. 9749. Victor S/S Cat. No. 89051. D/S Cat. No. 8012A. H.M.V. S/S Cat. No. 2-054094. D/S Cat. No. D.M. 111. German Cat. Nos. 78523 and 78522.

This record was also only issued in England in May, 1920, but then kept its place on the H.M.V. General Catalogue until 1946. After 1923 it was backed in this country by the "Don Carlos" duet with Scotti made in December, 1912, but as a Victor double sided record, by the "Già i sacerdoti adunansi" and in this form was re-issued as one of the Heritage series—as 15-1025. It remained on general release in U.S.A. from March, 1911 until 1928. In Germany it had the same backing as in U.S.A.

These two records of the great duet at the commencement of the 4th Act of Aida, are again splendidly sung, and it must be admitted that good as Caruso is, he is partnered by a Homer who is at the very peak of her form, and who carries all before her. Her range is exceptional, for she sings the top "B's" excellently, and altogether is most dramatic and convincing.

The following five records were made in Camden on November 19th, 1911

BALLO IN MASCHERA (Verdi) "Dì tu se fedele" (with chorus).

> Matrix No. 11270. Victor S/S Cat. No. 87091. D/S Cat. No. 512A. H.M.V. S/S Cat. No. 7-52025. D/S Cat. No. D.A. 102 German Cat. Nos. 74532 and 80009.

This record made its appearance in England in April, 1912. In 1923 it was backed by the 1908 "Questa o quella" and remained in this form on the H.M.V. General Catalogue until 1946. As a Victor double sided disc it was coupled with the 1906 "Di quella pira" from "Il Trovatore", and remained there on general release from December, 1911 until 1930. As a German double sided record, its backing was the same as in this country.

This is not the very best Caruso. Perhaps it is the recording, but the voice sounds hard, and a little tight, and although the whole is sung with fine rhythmic energy and style, there is little chance for Caruso to display his legato, or the finer points of phrasing. The chorus is so weak and so thin, as to be worse than none at all.

"Core'ngrato" (Carolli).

> Matrix No. 11274. Victor S/S Cat. No. 88334. D/S Cat. No. 6032A. H.M.V. S/S Cat. No. 2-052060. D/S Cat. No. D.B. 142. German Cat. No. 85029.

Issued in England in 1913 (June), this record remained on the H.M.V. General Catalogue in single sided form until it was backed by "Santa Lucia", and is now one of the few original Caruso recordings still to retain its place in the General Catalogue of 1954-55. As a Victor double sided record it had the same coupling as in this country and was available from December, 1911 until 1933. In Germany as a double sided record it was backed by "Fenesta che lucive".

In this recording we can realize how fine an interpreter of his native songs Caruso was. The air is now so familiar as to be thoroughly hackneyed, but there is no doubt he brings freshness to it, and a haunting melancholy which is most attractive, while the high notes ring out well.

BOHEME (Leoncavallo) "Testa adorata".

> Matrix No. 11272. Victor S/S Cat. No. 88331. D/S Cat. No. 6012B. H.M.V. S/S Cat. No. 2-052059. D/S Cat. No. D.B. 122. German Cat. Nos. 76103, 76102 and 85028.

This record was isued here in November, 1912 with the title from this opera "Io non ho che una povera stanzetta" recorded later in the month being released at the same time. It remained on the H.M.V. General Catalogue in single sided form until 1923, when it became one side of H.M.V. D.B. 122, until its deletion at the end of June, 1951. In U.S.A. it was issued in December, 1911—some two months earlier than its companion record, and was available until 1928. In Germany it was backed with the other aria from the same opera, as it was in U.S.A.

This aria is very well done and there is no doubt that Caruso must have liked this less familiar version of the well known story. He sings this aria with great feeling and unfailingly beautiful tone. In the absence of a score it is difficult to say more, but this is undoubtedly one of the finest things Caruso did in this particular session.

LO SCHIAVO (Gomez) "Quando nascesti tu".

Matrix No. 11273. Victor S/S Cat. No. 88345. D/S Cat. No. 6027B. H.M.V. S/S Cat. No. 2-052062. D/S Cat. No. D.B. 137. German Cat. Nos. 76015 and 85031.

Not issued in England until June, 1913, this record was transferred to the H.M.V. No. 2 List in 1926, and remained there until its deletion in 1941. Both as D.B. 137 and as a double sided Victor record it was coupled with the "Ballo in Maschera" aria "Ma se m'è forza perderti". It was on general release as a Victor record from September, 1912 until 1928. Its coupling as a German record was the same as here and in U.S.A.

This is interesting as it contains the recitative and also because it has not often been recorded. It starts quite lyrically, but some of the high notes towards the end are not reached with quite the ease which had been apparent in the earlier recordings. Nevertheless it is an excellent disc, and quite representative of Caruso at this period.

"Eternamente" (Mascheroni).

Matrix No. 11271. Victor S/S Cat. No. 88333. D/S Cat. No. 6034A. H.M.V. S/S Cat. No. 2-052058. D/S Cat. No. D.B. 121. German Cat. Nos. 76161 and 85042.

Issued here in April, 1912, this record remained in single sided form on the H.M.V. General Catalogue until its transferrence as D.B. 121 to the No. 2 List in 1924. It was deleted in 1941. In England it was coupled with "Manella mia" but as a Victor disc it had the 1919 recorded "Mia piccirella" on the reverse side. It was re-issued in the H.M.V. Archive series in 1951 as V.B. 60, with the 1908 "Lolita" on the other side. "Lolita" was also its companion as a German record. It was available in U.S.A. from December, 1911 until 1928.

Just why Caruso thought it necessary to record this typical Victorian drawing room ballad, it is difficult to say. He sings it with gusto, and seems to enjoy himself, and there is no doubt that he has given enjoyment through it to thousands of English speaking people, who are more familiar with it in the English version, known as "For all eternity". There is some rough singing towards the end, where the great tenor's tone is anything but beautiful, and it is perhaps as well that this recording does not go on "eternamente".

The following five records were made in Camden on November 26th, 1911

"Canta pe'me" (De Curtis).

> Matrix No. 11306. Victor S/S Cat. No. 87092. D/S Cat. No. 502B. H.M.V. S/S Cat. No. 7-52026. D/S Cat. No. D.A. 104. German Cat. Nos. 74533 and 80016.

This record was over two years reaching this country, being issued here in December, 1913. It then remained on the H.M.V. General Catalogue in single sided form until 1923, and afterwards in double sided form until 1946. Both here and in U.S.A. it was backed by "Addio a Napoli" but in Germany "Pimpinella" formed the reverse side. It was available from February, 1912 until 1940, in U.S.A.

This record is only of interest to those who like Caruso, no matter what he is singing. The Neapolitan song here recorded is without the obvious charm of many of the species, and although Caruso sings it quite well, it fails to charm. He makes excellent use of tempo rubato, without ever being vulgar, and his turns are models of neatness.

BOHEME (Leoncavallo) "Io non ho che una povera stanzetta".

> Matrix No. 11276. Victor S/S Cat. No. 88335. D/S Cat. No. 6012A. H.M.V. S/S Cat. No. 2-052061. D/S Cat. No. D.B. 122. German Cat. Nos. 76104 and 85028.

This record was issued here exactly twelve months after its recording in New York, and remained on the H.M.V. General Catalogue in single sided form until 1923 and then as D.B. 122 until its deletion at the end of June, 1951. Both here, in U.S.A., and in Germany it was originally backed by the "Testa adorata" recorded a week earlier, but when it was recently re-issued in America, in the Heritage Series as

15-1038, it was coupled with the 1916 recorded Macbeth aria "Ah, la paterna mano". It was on the Victor list from February, 1912 until 1928.

There is no doubt that Caruso must have liked this less familiar version of the well known story. It is the companion piece to the aria recorded a week earlier, and the same qualities noted then are equally apparent here. Together the arias form an extremely attractive double sided record, for while Caruso's singing is of the highest standard, there is the added attraction of having a recording of two arias which are unlikely to be repeated.

LA FORZA DEL DESTINO (Verdi) "Invano Alvaro" (with Amato).

Matrix No. 11286. Victor S/S Cat. No. 89052. D/S Cat. No. 8005A. H.M.V. S/S Cat. No. 2-054027. D/S Cat. No. D.M. 106. German Cat. No. 78526.

This duet was issued in England in March, 1912 and, as did all but three of Caruso's records, ceased to be available in single sided form in 1923. It then became one side of D.M. 106 with "Le minaccie i fieri accenti" on the reverse side, and was deleted in 1946, when the general slaughter of Caruso's concerted numbers took place. Its coupling in U.S.A. was the same as in England, as it also was in Germany. It remained on general release as a Victor record from December, 1911 until 1928.

(For review, see the following record).

LA FORZA DEL DESTINO (Verdi) "Le minaccie i fieri accenti" (with Amato).

Matrix No. 11286½. Victor S/S Cat. No. 89053. D/S Cat. No. 8005B. H.M.V. S/S Cat. No. 2-054028. D/S Cat. No. D.M. 106. German Cat. Nos. 78526 and 78527.

This, like the first part of the duet described above, was issued here in March, 1912, became double sided in 1923, and was deleted in 1946. Both here, in U.S.A. and Germany it was coupled with the "Invano Alvaro". It was on general release in U.S.A. from December, 1911 until 1928.

This recording strikes a happy balance between the demands of bel canto singing, and the dramatic excess of some later interpretations. Both Caruso and Amato are in excellent voice, and the rapid phrases of the concluding dialogue are excellently handled, and provide a fine example of controlled declamation.

L'ELISIR D'AMORE (Donizetti) "Una furtiva lagrima".

Matrix No. 996. Victor S/S Cat. No. 88339. D/S Cat. No. 6016A. H.M.V. S/S Cat. No. 2-052064. D/S Cat. No. D.B. 126. German Cat. Nos. 76106 and 85012.

The odd-looking matrix number is of course the result of conforming it to that of the two 1904 discs, only the letter of the alphabet preceding the numerals distinguishing the three discs. The same thing happened with the 1906 and 1917 recordings of the romance from Marta. This is the only recording of this aria made by Caruso, which had orchestral accompaniment. It made its appearance in England in September, 1913 and remained on the H.M.V. General List for about eleven years, and was then transferred to the No. 2 Catalogue, on its first issue in 1924, as D.B. 126, backed by the Rigoletto aria "Parmi veder le lagrime", where it held its place until 1942. As a Victor double sided disc it had the same coupling as in this country. It was reissued as a Victor record in 1951 in a "Special Request Catalogue" with the original coupling. It was available in U.S.A. from March, 1912 until 1952. In Germany it was backed by "Che gelida manina" (La Bohème).

This is a straightforward rendering of this favourite aria, and lacks the style of the earlier ones. There is no attempt to emulate the tour de force of the second verse recording of 1904, and in fact save for the remarkable agility shown in the cadenza, one would not realize that Caruso was so far ahead of his nearest rivals, by listening to this disc. Bonci, McCormack, and many others have sung the aria better than this. None however has equalled the splendid singing of the earlier Victor recording.

The following four records were made in Camden on December 27th, 1911.

AIDA (Verdi) "Celeste Aida".

Matrix No. 11423. Victor S/S Cat. No. 88127. D/S Cat. No. 6000A. H.M.V. S/S Cat. No. 2-052066. D/S Cat. No. D.K. 115. German Cat. Nos. 76108 and 85022.

The last of Caruso's five recordings of this aria (and the only one preceded by the recitative "Se quel guerrier io fossi"), had an unusual history so far as this country is concerned. The first mention of it which we have been able to trace, is in the International Artists' Celebrity Records Catalogue, January, 1914. It is not to be found in the special Caruso brochure issued in October, 1921, two months after the singer's death, and it seems never to have found a place in the H.M.V. General Catalogue until 1922, though it had been available for some years in U.S.A. It had a very brief life on the H.M.V. General Catalogue for the last mention of it there is in 1924. In November of that year, the No. 2 Catalogue of Historic Records made its first appearance and 2-052066 is at once found there in double sided form as D.K. 115, backed by the first part of the Judgment Hall duet from "Aida" which Caruso made with Louise Homer just twelve months previously. It remained on the No. 2 List until its deletion in 1946. As a Victor double sided disc it was coupled with the "O tu che in seno agli angeli" recorded in November, 1909, and was available from 1912 until 1952. In Germany it had the same coupling as it had in U.S.A.

This is the last of the recordings of the aria made by Caruso, and in some ways it is the best. The voice is not so beautiful as in the earlier recordings, and it does not rise with the effortless ease of former years, but it does declaim the opening recitative quite magnificently, and the phrasing of the aria, as in the 1908 version is more orthodox. The final B flat is excellent, and not too robust.

MANON (Massenet) **"Ah fuyez douce image"** (preceded by recitative, "Je suis seul").

> Matrix No. 11422. Victor S/S Cat. No. 88348. D/S Cat. No. 6020B. H.M.V. S/S Cat. No. 2-032005. D/S Cat. No. D.B. 130. German Cat. Nos. 76017 and 85004.

Issued in England in June, 1913, this record remained on the H.M.V. General Catalogue in singled sided form until 1924, when it was transferred as D.B. 130 to the No. 2 Historic List, and was backed by the French version of the "Carmen" Flower Song recorded in November, 1909. It was deleted in 1942. As a Victor double sided disc, it originally had the final recording of "Cielo e mar" on its reverse side, but when in recent years it was re-issued as one of the Heritage series— 15-1004—it was coupled with the La Juive aria, recorded in 1920. It remained on general release in U.S.A. from April, 1912 until 1930. In Germany as a double sided disc, it was coupled with "Salut demeure" (Faust).

The better the machine, the better this recording sounds, and there is no doubt that it is very fine in many respects. There is some slight sign of effort in the trying concluding phrases, but the opening recitative, and the more reflective passages, are in Caruso's best manner and his line is well nigh perfect. Considering the high tessitura, and the date of this recording, this is a fine example of the singer's voice at this period of his career.

BALLO IN MASCHERA (Verdi) "Ma se m'è forza perderti".

Matrix No. 11420. Victor S/S Cat. No. 88346. D/S Cat. No. 6027A. H.M.V. S/S Cat. No. 2-052065. D/S Cat. No. D.B. 137. German Cat. Nos. 76107 and 85031.

This record was issued in England only in June, 1913 and then remained as a single sided record on the H.M.V. General Catalogue until 1924, when as D.B. 137 it was backed by the Gomez aria from "Lo Schiavo". Two years later it was transferred to the No. 2 Historic List, and remained there until its deletion in 1941. Both as a Victor and German double sided record it had the same coupling as here. It was on the Victor Catalogue from January, 1913 until 1928.

There is no denying the authority of this singing, but at the same time there is a tendency to declaim all the time, and the composer's markings are largely ignored. The tone is also rather hard, and the alterations in the final cadenza, although customary, seem rather superfluous. This then, is good orthodox singing, but by no means one of the outstanding examples of Caruso's art.

"Love is Mine" (Gartner).

Matrix No. 11419. Victor S/S Cat. No. 87095. D/S Cat. No. 510A. H.M.V. S/S Cat. No. 4-2205. D/S Cat. No. D.A. 111. German Cat. Nos. 74501 and 80000.

Caruso's second essay in English was issued here in 1912 (June). It ceased to be a single sided record in 1924, and was then backed by Tchaikovsky's "Pourquoi". It was deleted from the General Catalogue in 1941. As a Victor double sided disc, it was coupled with Tosti's "Parted", and was on general release from April, 1912 until 1924. In Germany it was backed by "For you alone".

This is quite a pleasing ordinary ballad, and Caruso sings it in quite reasonable English. Why his choice lighted upon this particular example of the genus, it would be hard to say, but no doubt it has been very popular. There are some well sustained high notes.

The following six records were made in New York on January 7th, 1912

MARTA (Flotow) **"Siam giunto o giovinette"** (with Alda, Jacoby and Journet).

Matrix No. 11437. Victor S/S Cat. No. 95207. D/S Cat. No. 10002A. H.M.V. S/S Cat. No. 2-054030. D/S Cat. No. D.M. 100. German Cat. No. 78528.

The first mention of this record in England which we have been able to trace is in the International Celebrity Artists' Catalogue which came out in January, 1914. It remained in the H.M.V. General Catalogue in single sided form until 1924, when it was backed by the "Che vuol dir ciò?" as D.M. 100, and remained on the catalogue until 1946. As a Victor double sided disc its coupling was the same as here. It was issued in June, 1912 and remained on the Victor General Catalogue until 1927. In Germany it was coupled with the "T'ho raggiunta sciagurata".

(For review see paragraph at the end of the series of four recordings.)

MARTA (Flotow) **"Che vuol dir ciò"** (with Alda, Jacoby, Journet).

Matrix No. 11438. Victor S/S Cat. No. 95208. D/S Cat. No. 10002B. H.M.V. S/S Cat. No. 2-054031. D/S Cat. No. D.M. 100. German Cat. No. 78529.

The history of this record in England is identical with that just reviewed—2-054030. Its coupling in U.S.A. was the same as in England, but there it was issued in the June following its recording, and was deleted in 1927, nearly twenty years before its disappearance in this country. As a German double sided record it was coupled with the "Presto presto" quartet from the same opera.

(For review see paragraph at the end of the series of four recordings).

MARTA (Flotow) **"Presto, presto andiam"** (with Alda, Jacoby and Journet).

Matrix No. 11439. Victor S/S Cat. No. 95209. D/S Cat. No. 10003A. H.M.V. S/S Cat. No. 2-054032. D/S Cat. No. D.M. 101. German Cat. Nos. 78530 and 78529.

The history of this record in England is identical with that of the two just reviewed. Its coupling as a Victor double sided disc was the "T'ho raggiunta sciagurata" or "Goodnight quartet" as it was in this country. As with the other three quartets it was available to the American public in June, 1912 and did not disappear until 1930. In Germany it was coupled with the "Che vuol dir cio" quartet.

(For review see paragraph at the end of the series of four recordings).

72

MARTA (Flotow) **"T'ho raggiunta sciagurata"** (with Alda, Jacoby and Journet).

Matrix No. 11440. Victor S/S Cat. No. 95210. D/S Cat. No. 10003B. H.M.V. S/S Cat. No. 2-054037. D/S Cat. No. D.M. 101. German S/S Cat. No. 78531. D/S Cat. No. 78528.

This, the most popular number of these four Marta quartets, was issued in England in November, 1912. After 1923 it was coupled with the "Presto presto, andiam" and remained as a double sided record on the General Catalogue until 1946. It was issued in U.S.A. in June, 1912 and deleted in 1930. It had the same coupling in U.S.A. as in England, but in Germany it was backed by the "Siam giunti o giovinetti" quartet.

Caruso was in excellent voice when these four quartets were recorded and they form a delightful set. "Siam giunti" contains a rather long orchestral introduction, but the concerted singing is excellent. All is light and cheerful, and the music gives no hint of the irony the girls feel. "Che vuol dir cio" contains some pleasant lyrical singing but is the least interesting of the four sides. "Presto, presto andiam" is sprightly in the extreme, and Alda shines in some neat coloratura passages towards the end. The ensemble is excellent. "T'ho raggiunta" sciagurata" is chiefly notable for Caruso's superb singing of the solo "Dormi pure". His lyrical perfection recalls vividly his singing of earlier years, and in fact the second of these two records—D.M. 101—is in every way an excellent coupling, but the whole set is very strongly recommended.

"Crucifix" (Faure) (with Journet).

Matrix No. 11442. Victor S/S Cat. No. 89054. D/S Cat. No. 6347A. H.M.V. S/S Cat. No. 2-034013. D/S Cat. No. D.B. 591. German Cat. No. 78504.

This record of Gabriel Faure's well-known sacred song was available here in April, 1912. It became D.B. 591 in 1923, when it was backed by another Faure song "Les Rameaux" sung by the great French bass Pol Plançon, and the same coupling was used in U.S.A. and Germany. It remained on the H.M.V. General List until 1941, but in U.S.A. it was only available from March, 1912 until 1924. In this country, in its double sided form, it only had the red label which belonged to Caruso's solo records, (as did the duet with De Gogorza "A la luz de la luna" and the duet with Destinn, "Sento una forza indomita"), and retailed at a lower price than in its original form, when it had the light green label.

73

Again Caruso is in excellent voice, and he is partnered by that most reliable of French basses, Marcel Journet. The singing throughout is of a very high order, with a most perfect legato maintained throughout. There are some fine high notes at the conclusion, and the concerted passages are exceptionally good.

I LOMBARDI (Verdi) "Qual voluttà trascorrere" (with Alda and Journet).

> Matrix No. 11441. Victor S/S Cat. No. 95211. D/S Cat. No. 10010A. H.M.V. S/S Cat. No. 2-054029. D/S Cat. No. D.M. 126. German S/S Cat. No. 78542. D/S Cat. No. 78539.

This record, one of the greatest triumphs of pre-electrical recording, was issued in this country in June, 1912. In 1923, it was backed by the "Samson and Delilah" Trio "Je viens célébrer la victoire" and as D.M. 126 remained on the General Catalogue until 1946. In U.S.A. it was issued in March, 1912, backed by the same trio as in England, but was withdrawn as early as 1927. As a continental record, it was backed by the "Faust" Trio "Que voulez-vous messieurs".

All three singers sound extremely healthy in this excellent recording. Apart from the fact that the tenor is supposed to be dying, there is no cause for criticism. To tell the truth, Caruso demonstrates most conclusively that his lungs are in the most perfect condition, and this exceptionally fine recording is most strongly recommended.

The following two records were made in New York on January 19th, 1912

"Tarantella Sincera" (Crescenzo).

> Matrix No. 11472. Victor S/S Cat. No. 88347. D/S Cat. No. 6031B. H.M.V. S/S Cat. No. 2-052067. D/S Cat. No. D.B. 141. German Cat. Nos. 76109 and 85035.

Caruso's only comic song, which has as its subject an unhappy bachelor vainly searching for a wife sufficiently domesticated to satisfy him, was issued in England in July, 1912, and taking its place then on the General Catalogue remained there until the end of 1952. After 1923 as a double sided disc, it was backed by "La Danza" (Rossini) recorded in February, 1912. As a Victor and also a German disc, it had the same coupling. It was on general release in U.S.A. from April, 1912 until 1928.

Again this is a trifle, musically, but few will be able to resist the artist's infectious gaiety. The tune will not bear endless repetition, either, but when it has not been heard for some time, it is exceedingly pleasant. The singing is lively in the extreme, and the high notes are beautifully taken.

LUCIA DI LAMMERMOOR (Donizetti) **"Chi mi frena"** (with Tetrazzini, Amato, Journet, Bada and Jacoby).
> Matrix No. 11446. Only Victor Cat. No. 96201. Only H.M.V. Cat. No. 2-054034.

This record, as far as we have been able to ascertain, has only appeared in single sided form, (except for its appearance in the "Metropolitan Revivals" series), and not even in that form on the Continent. It was over 11 years in making its appearance here, in the H.M.V. monthly supplement for February, 1923, so that as far as this country is concerned it is a posthumous record—easily the earliest recorded of all Caruso's posthumously issued recordings. It retained its place on the H.M.V. General Catalogue until 1946. In the U.S.A. however, it was issued in April, 1912, three months after its recording, and was deleted in 1927.

The various voices stand out quite clearly in the first half of this record, but there is a tendency for them to merge into one close texture towards the close. Tetrazzini emits one or two excellent high notes, and Caruso is well to the fore—perhaps a little too much so for an ideal ensemble, but this is first rate entertainment value.

The following two records were made in New York on February 13th, 1912

RIGOLETTO (Verdi) **"Bella figlia dell'amore"** (with Tetrazzini, Amato and Jacoby).
> Matrix No. 11447. Only H.M.V. Cat. No. 2-054038. German Cat. No. 79003.

This record has had an highly irregular history. It has never been listed on any English H.M.V. Catalogue, any records of it obtained here being either special pressings or imported from abroad. Nor was it on regular Victor release, the International Record Collectors' Club being first responsible for circulating copies of it to its members in the U.S.A. as I.R.C.C. 36, backed by the "Ebben qual nuovo fremito" duet from Aida, sung by Destinn and Kirkby Lunn. Later it was issued in

U.S.A. in the Heritage Series as 15-1019, with the Melba, McCormack and Sammarco trio from Faust, on the reverse side. It seems to have been for some time on regular release in Germany, with the Catalogue Number 79003, with the Sextet from "Lucia di Lammermoor" in which Sembrich sings Lucy's part, on the reverse side. It may interest collectors to know that on the special pressing done at Hayes for the writer many years ago, the following can be clearly read, etched beneath the yellow label. Against the dog's head the letter "E"; Half way down its body "C 11447"; immediately under its feet "Feb 13-12". On a level with this but to the left of the hole in the centre of the record is seen the numeral "4". Just below the "Feb 13-12" are the numerals "10195" "Quartette Rigoletto" "Tetrazzini—Jacoby—Caruso—Amata". On the record itself is embossed "A 11447".

The reason for the non-issue of this version in England is not clear. Admittedly Caruso's introductory solo is not so good as in the earlier versions, but it is very fine, the ensemble singing is better recorded and the voices although excellently blended, stand out well from each other. Tetrazzini is excellent throughout.

"La Danza" (Rossini).

> Matrix No. 11590. Victor S/S Cat. No. 88355. D/S Cat. No. 6031A. H.M.V. S/S Cat. No. 2-052068. D/S Cat. No. D.B. 141. German S/S Cat. No. 76110. D/S Cat. No. 85035. Later in Victor Heritage Series, on vinylite only issued in U.S.A., 15-1040.

This record made its appearance here in October, 1912 and when in 1923 Caruso's records became double sided, it was backed by "Tarantella Sincera" as D.B. 141, and was only withdrawn on January 31st, 1955. In the U.S.A. and on the Continent it had the same backing, but the Heritage series had "Fenesta che lucive" on the reverse side. It was first issued in U.S.A. in May, 1912 and withdrawn in 1928.

This is sung a little roughly, but with tremendous élan, and the rhythm is so firm and so unrelenting that there are few if any modern versions to touch this spirited rendering.

Recorded April 18th, 1912. Camden

"Dreams of long ago" (Caruso).

> Matrix No. 11616. Victor S/S Cat. No. 88376. D/S Cat. No. 6015A. H.M.V. S/S Cat. No. 02396. D/S Cat. No. D.B. 125. German S/S Cat. No. 76000. D/S Cat. No. 85001.

This is Caruso's third essay in English and he himself is credited with the waltz time music. (It was once issued as a waltz, played by the Black Diamonds Band, on a 10 inch Zonophone record X-2-40475. Serial 2311). It took nearly two years to reach England, not making its appearance until March, 1914. In 1923 it became D.B. 125, backed by "Love me or not", and was not deleted from the H.M.V. General Catalogue until 1949. In U.S.A. it made its appearance in July of 1912, and was subsequently coupled with the same backing as here, being finally withdrawn in 1930. In its German form it was backed by "The Lost Chord".

It was naturally to be expected that Caruso should try his hand at the lighter type of composition, and it can quite honestly be said that it is no worse than similar effusions by other composers. Naturally it fits the singer's voice like a glove, and that voice is warm and ringing. The recording is excellent.

Recorded April 29th, 1912. Camden

"The Lost Chord" (Sullivan).

> Matrix No. 11942. Victor S/S Cat. No. 88378. D/S Cat. No. 6023B. H.M.V. S/S Cat. No. 02397. D/S Cat. No. D.B. 133. German S/S Cat. No. 76001. D/S Cat. No. 85001.

This record in English was quickly made available here, being issued in September, 1912. It became a double sided record in 1923, with Handel's "Largo" on the reverse side, and kept its place on the H.M.V. Catalogue until June, 1951. In U.S.A. where it had the same backing as here, it was issued in July, 1912 and withdrawn in 1933. In its German form it was backed by "Dreams of long ago".

As a demonstration of Caruso's amazing resonance at this period of his career, this record is a great success. In any case it was inevitable !

The following two records were made in New York on December 7th, 1912

"Because" (Guy d'Hardelot).

> Matrix No. 12680. Victor S/S Cat. No. 87122. D/S Cat. No. 506A. H.M.V. S/S Cat. No. 7-32004. D/S Cat. No. D.A. 107. German S/S Cat. No. 74503. D/S Cat. No. 80002.

Over three years elapsed between the recording of this song and its issue here in May, 1916. When it became a double sided record in

1923 it had Szulc's "Hantise d'amour" on the reverse side. It was finally deleted in 1941. In U.S.A. it was on general release from February, 1913 until 1927, with the same backing as a double sided disc as it had here, but in its German form it had Tosti's "Pour un baiser" on the reverse side.

This is sung in French, and is not really a satisfactory performance. There is too much effort, and it is sung too operatically. There is a very big deterioration to be noted in the vocal quality of this recording when compared with the Manon duet of the same month.

"Hosanna" (Granier).

> Matrix No. 12681. Victor S/S Cat. No. 88403. D/S Cat. No. 6022A. H.M.V. S/S Cat. No. 2-032008. D/S Cat. No. D.B. 132. German S/S Cat. No. 76018. D/S Cat. No. 85008.

This record was issued in England in April, 1914 and remained on the General Catalogue (as students of Caruso's recordings will notice did most of his later records) throughout its history. It became D.B. 132 in 1923 with "Les Rameaux" on the reverse side and was deleted in 1941. It was in print from February, 1913, in U.S.A., being deleted in 1928. Caruso's records were, with very few exceptions withdrawn much earlier in U.S.A. than they were here and this was the case with this record. Both in U.S.A. and under its German label it had the same backing as in this country.

A forward recording, in which the great Italian's high notes simply peal out. There is tremendous energy used, and the singing is not without signs of effort. The music is trite.

The following three records were made in New York on December 30th, 1912

MANON (Massenet) **"On l'appelle Manon"** (with Farrar).

> Matrix No. 12750. Victor S/S Cat. No. 89059. D/S Cat. No. 8011B. H.M.V. S/S Cat. No. 2-034018. D/S Cat. No. D.M. 110. German S/S Cat. No. 78505. D/S Cat. No. 78515.

This record, as was the case with so many of Caruso's concerted numbers, took nearly two and a half years to reach this country, not being issued here until May, 1915. In 1923 it was backed by the lovely Butterfly duet with Farrar, ("O quanti occhi fisi"), and was not deleted before 1946. Both as a Victor and a German record it had the same backing as here, and it remained on the Victor list from March, 1913 until 1928.

This is a relief after the stentorian efforts displayed in the record previously reviewed. Caruso is back into his most lyrical vein and sings this delightful music with the utmost charm. He is partnered to perfection by Geraldine Farrar, who is never heard to better advantage than when singing with Caruso.

LA BOHEME (Puccini) "**O soave fanciulla**" (with Farrar).

> Matrix No. 12751. I.R.C.C. Cat. No. 61B.

It is to the enterprise of the International Record Collectors' Club that we owe the issue of this record in 1936, twenty-four years after its recording. It has apparently never been released on regular issue in America, England, or on the Continent. It was issued by I.R.C.C. as a double sided record with the well-known "Mi par d'udir" from "The Pearl Fishers", which Caruso had made in Milan in 1903, on the reverse side.

Unfortunately this recording is very inferior, from the tenor's point of view, to his wonderful singing in the duet with Melba, recorded in 1907. While he still sings well, the voice as recorded has lost some of the bloom, and the high notes are reached with a sense of effort which is conspicuously absent from the earlier recording. Farrar sings well, and the balance of the two voices is better in this disc.

DON CARLOS (Verdi) "**Dio che nell'alma infondere**" (with Scotti).

> Matrix No. 12752. Victor S/S Cat. No. 89064. D/S Cat. No. 8036B. H.M.V. S/S Cat. No. 2-054095. D/S Cat. No. D.M. 111. German S/S and D/S Cat. No. 78533.

This record is the last of the many in which he is associated with his friend Scotti. It was nearly three years in reaching this country, making its appearance in the H.M.V. October, 1915 monthly supplement with great éclat, and a photograph of the two singers listening together to its reproduction. It became a double sided disc in 1923 as D.M. 111, having on its reverse side the Caruso-Homer rendering of "Aida a me togliesti". It was not deleted from the General Catalogue until 1946. As a Victor record, it was listed from April, 1913 until 1928 and was backed by the Pearl Fishers duet "Del tempio al limitar". Under its German label it had the Caruso-Ruffo duet from Otello (Si pel ciel) on the reverse side.

Although this is the last recording in which Scotti joins Caruso, it is not the best, for the dramatic intensity of the singing is gained by the sacrifice of smoothness, and there is some blasting. It is nevertheless a fine rendering, and well worth possessing.

The following two records were made in New York on January 17th, 1913

IL TROVATORE (Verdi) **"Ai nostri monti ritorneremo"** (with Schumann-Heink).

> Matrix No. 12804. Victor S/S Cat. No. 89060. D/S Cat. No. 8042B. H.M.V. S/S Cat. No. 2-054042. D/S Cat. No. D.K. 119. German S/S Cat. No. 78532. D/S Cat. No. 78518.

This is the third and final rendering of the famous duet, and it took over seven years to reach England, being issued here between April and December of 1920. In 1923 it became D.K. 119, and five years later was transferred to the No. 2 List, with the equally well-known "Miserere" with Alda, on the other side. It was not deleted until 1946. In U.S.A. with the same backing as here, (as it also had in Germany) it was on issue from April 1913 until 1953—a long history for a Caruso record in U.S.A.

Caruso's voice is noticeably less lyrical than in the earlier of the two versions with Homer. He sings more dramatically, and the effect might well be more telling in the theatre, but as pure singing this version is inferior to the first one, with its wonderful breath control. He does not insert a high note at the end as in the later version with Homer.

Schumann Heink sings very well, and is less constricted than Homer, but this is by no means one of her best records. Nevertheless the voices blend well, and the record is well worth acquiring, without being as outstanding as it might have been.

"Pimpinella" (Tchaikowsky) (piano accompaniment).

> Matrix No. 12805. Victor S/S Cat. No. 87128. D/S Cat. No. 518A. H.M.V. S/S Cat. No. 7-52038. D/S Cat. No. D.A. 119. German S/S Cat. No. 74538. D/S Cat. No. 80016.

Issued in England in April, 1914, it retained its place as a single sided disc until 1923, when as D.A. 119, it was coupled with "Vieni sul mar". It remained on the General Catalogue until 1941, when it was deleted. As a Victor disc, it was in print from April, 1913, until 1930, with the same backing as it had here, but as a German record it had "Canta pe' me" on the reverse side.

This is an undistinguished song, sung in an undistinguished way. It gives little idea of Caruso's powers, and is not particularly well recorded. I advise only the specialist collector to worry with it. One small point of interest is the power of the low "C" or "C" sharp which Caruso sings, with considerable resonance, but a true tenor quality.

The following three records were made in New York on February 24th, 1913

RIGOLETTO (Verdi) **"Parmi veder le lagrime".**

> Matrix No. 11421. Victor S/S Cat. No. 88429. D/S Cat. No. 6016B. H.M.V. S/S Cat. No. 2-052076. D/S Cat. No. D.B. 126. German S/S Cat. No. 76111. D/S Cat. No. 85019.

Issued here in April 1914, this record passed the whole of its single sided life on the H.M.V. General Catalogue, and then in 1923 it appeared on the No. 2 List, as D.B. 126 with Caruso's final recording of "Una furtiva lagrima" on the reverse side, and was finally deleted in 1942. In U.S.A. with the same backing as a double sided record, it was in circulation from June, 1913 until 1952. As a German record, it was backed by "Ah si ben mio coll'essere" from Il Trovatore.

What a pity Caruso did not record this five or six years earlier. It shows some signs of strain, and the end betrays difficulty with the tessitura. At the same time, the singer does make considerable use of a mezza voce, which was still under complete control. The singing, is however, too dramatic for the character of the Duke, and again, the recording is not very kind.

"Agnus Dei" (Bizet).

> Matrix No. 12942. Victor S/S Cat. No. 88425. D/S Cat. No. 6010A. H.M.V. S/S Cat. No. 02470. D/S Cat. No. D.B. 120. German S/S Cat. No. 76002. D/S Cat. No. 85003.

Issued in England in December, 1914, this record became double sided as D.B. 120 in 1923, with "Domine Deus" as its companion. It remained on the General Catalogue until its deletion in 1941. In U.S.A. with the same backing as here, it was on general release from May, 1913 until 1930. Under its German label it was backed not very appropriately by Tosti's "Ideale".

The recording is better here, and the wonderful melody finely sung in the opening phrases. The high B flats at the close show very great signs of effort, and the general tone of the rendering is much too emotional or theatrical for English tastes.

MANON LESCAUT (Puccini) **"Donna non vidi mai".**

Matrix No. 12945. Victor S/S Cat. No. 87135. D/S Cat. No. 505A. H.M.V. S/S Cat. No. 7-52039. D/S Cat. No. D.A. 106. German S/S Cat. No. 74539. D/S Cat. No. 80013.

It is surprising that this record should be the only one made by Caruso from this opera, for by general consent the role of Des Grieux in Puccini's opera was one of his greatest parts. It was on the General Catalogue till its deletion in 1942, having been issued in June, 1914. As a double sided disc after 1923, it was coupled with "Guardann'a luna". As a Victor record it was in print from May, 1913 until 1930. Both in U.S.A. and Germany it was backed by the "Ora e per sempre addio" from Verdi's Otello.

Without question this is the best of the three recordings made in February, 1913. The voice sounds more free, and rings out well in the typical Puccini melody, which suits Caruso to perfection. On the whole though, he does not appear to have been in his best voice when this recording session took place.

The following two records were made in New York on March 20th, 1913

"Ave Maria" (Kahn) (with Mischa Elman—violin—and piano).

Matrix No. 13004. Victor S/S Cat. No. 89065. D/S Cat. No. 8007A. H.M.V. S/S Cat. No. 02472. D/S Cat. No. D.K. 103. German S/S Cat. No. 77500. D/S Cat. No. 85045.

Issued in England in October, 1913 and becoming a double sided record in 1923, this disc was not deleted from the General Catalogue until 1946. In this country, in U.S.A., and in Germany it had on its reverse side Massenet's "Elégie". Issued in U.S.A. in June, 1913, it remained in print there until 1951.

Although Caruso's voice sounds heavy in these recordings with Elman, it has a richness and a dark quality which are quite captivating, and it is used with much less sense of effort. This "Ave Maria" has a striking melody, and is well sung by Caruso.

82

"Elégie" (Massenet) (with Mischa Elman—violin—and piano).

> Matrix No. 13005. Victor S/S Cat. No. 89066. D/S Cat. No. 8007B.
> H.M.V. S/S Cat. No. 2-032010. D/S Cat. No. D.K. 103. German S/S
> Cat. No. 77502. D/S Cat. No. 85045.

Issued here in January, 1914, this record had exactly the same history as its companion record just reviewed. In U.S.A. it was available from 1913 (October) until 1951.

This recording is like the one just reviewed. The voice is dark and almost baritonal, but the great tenor sings the melody most movingly and this, combined with Elman's fine obligato, make the record most popular, and deservedly so. The French is not good.

The following four records were made in New York on April 10th, 1913

"Fenesta che lucive" (Unknown, but attributed to Bellini).

> Matrix No. 13107. Victor S/S Cat. No. 88439. D/S Cat. No. 6019A.
> H.M.V. S/S Cat. No. 2-052077. D/S Cat. No. D.B. 140. German S/S Cat.
> No. 76112. D/S Cat. No. 85029.

Not issued here until May, 1915, this record only remained on the H.M.V. General Catalogue as long as it retained its single sided form, and as D.B. 140 is only found on the No. 2 List, being present in the first issue of this Historic Catalogue which was in November, 1924 with the 1906 recording "Triste Ritorno" on the reverse side. It was deleted in 1941. As a Victor record, it was backed by "Ideale" and was available from November, 1913 until 1924. With its German label it had "Core 'n grato" on the reverse side.

This is sung with great feeling and good tone. The baritonal quality is less noticeable, and the recording rather more distant. The tune is a fine one, and is certainly reminiscent of Bellini, to whom it is attributed, and the record is a very pleasing one, especially for those who like Neapolitan Songs.

"Guardann'a luna" (Crescenzo).

> Matrix No. 13105. Victor S/S Cat. No. 87162. D/S Cat. No. 509A.
> H.M.V. S/S Cat. No. 7-52043. D/S Cat. No. D.A. 106. German S/S Cat.
> No. 74542. D/S Cat. No. 80020.

This record took over three years to reach England, not being available here until it appeared in the Monthly Supplementary List for May,

1916. In 1923 it became double sided with the Manon Lescaut aria
"Donna non vidi mai" on the reverse side, and finally disappeared
from the H.M.V. Catalogue in 1942. As a Victor record it was in
circulation from September, 1913 until 1927 with Leoncavallo's "Lasciati amar" on the reverse side. As a German double sided record, it
had Guy d'Hardelot's "Because" on the reverse side.

This is quite a pleasant melody of the lighter type, but it seems an
utter waste of Caruso's talents. No doubt it sold well, and was more
popular than some of the operatic records may have been. It is just
trivial, and is sung much better than it need be to be effective.

"Lasciati amar" (Leoncavallo).

> Matrix No. 13104. Victor S/S Cat. No. 87161. D/S Cat. No. 509B. H.M.V.
> S/S Cat. No. 7-52042. D/S Cat. No. D.A. 113. German S/S Cat. No.
> 74541. D/S Cat. No. 80019.

Dedicated to Caruso by its composer, this record made its appearance
in November, 1913. When Caruso's records became double sided in
1923, this recording, as D.A. 113 with the 1906 "Di quella pira" from
Il Trovatore on the reverse side was transferred to the No. 2 List in
its first issue of November, 1923, and was not deleted till 1946. Its
Victor coupling was "Guardann'a luna" and it was in circulation in
the U.S.A. from August, 1913 until 1927. In its German form it had
Ricciardi's "Amor mio" on the reverse side.

This is probably slightly more distinguished than the previous record,
and is well sung. Caruso's voice seems in much better fettle than it was
only two months previously.

"Your eyes have told me what I did not know". (O'Hara).

> Matrix No. 13106. Victor S/S Cat. No. 87159. D/S Cat. No. 514B.
> H.M.V. S/S Cat. No. 4-2375. D/S Cat. No. D.A. 115. German S/S Cat.
> No. 74599. D/S Cat. No. 80004.

Issued in England in December, 1914, this record remained on the
H.M.V. General Catalogue till its withdrawal in 1943, as did most of
Caruso's later recordings—and all those which he sang in English. It
became a double sided disc in 1923, with "Trusting eyes" on the reverse side. As a Victor record it had the same backing as here, as it
did also as a German record, and was listed in U.S.A. from July, 1913
until 1927.

We would draw attention to April being the actual date of this recording and not July which is wrongly attributed to it in previous Caruso discographies, including those done for the January, 1934 issue of "The Gramophone" and for the English edition of Dorothy Caruso's "Enrico Caruso—His life and Death". The compiler of these two catalogues owes an apology to students of the history of Caruso's records, for this error, which is the less excusable because Mr. Eric Bernard had already given him the correct date—April 10th, 1913. Probably the fact that July, 1913 was the date of issue of this record in U.S.A. led to the Victor Company giving him in 1933 that date as the date of recording. But there can be no doubt whatever as to the correct date. A perusal of pages 299-300 in Pierre Key's "Enrico Caruso" and pages 426-7 of the invaluable appendix to it compiled by Bruno Zirato, makes it quite clear that Caruso was not in U.S.A. during July, 1913 and of course there is no doubt about this recording having been made in New York.

Another inconsequential song, which Caruso sings really well. His voice seems to have been improving steadily throughout the early months of 1913, and his top notes are now much more easily produced once again.

The following three records were made in New York on December 15th, 1913

STABAT MATER (Rossini) "Cujus animam".

> Matrix No. 14200. Victor S/S Cat. No. 88460. D/S Cat. No. 6028B. H.M.V. S/S Cat. No. 2-052086. D/S Cat. No. D.B. 138. German S/S Cat. No. 76114. D/S Cat. No. 85027.

This record was issued here in April, 1915 and remained on the General Catalogue until its deletion in 1950. After 1923 as D.B. 138 it was backed by the "Ingemisco" from Verdi's Requiem. In U.S.A. where it was available from September, 1914 until 1933, it had the same backing as in this country, but as a German double sided disc it had Tosti's "Addio" on the reverse side.

Caruso's handling of the difficult phrasing of the opening bars is very fine. The long ascending passage in the middle causes him some trouble, and the high "C" sharp at the close is probably falsetto. The recording is not sufficiently good to be certain of this, but the note is most assuredly white, and lacks resonance. The whole atmosphere is rather theatrical, but it is in keeping with the music.

CAVALLERIA RUSTICANA (Mascagni) **"Addio alla madre"**.

Matrix No. 14202. Victor S/S Cat. No. 88458. D/S Cat. No. 6008B. H.M.V. S/S Cat. No. 2-052083. D/S Cat. No. D.B. 118. German S/S Cat. No. 76113. D/S Cat. No. 85020.

Not issued in England until June, 1916, this record retained its place on the H.M.V. General Catalogue until its deletion in 1942. It was coupled in 1923 with the Macbeth aria "Ah la paterna mano" and issued as D.B. 118. The Victor record which was listed from February, 1914 until 1933 had "Un di all'azzurro" as its companion, while the German one was backed by the 1908 "Celeste Aida".

The recording is greatly improved, and the voice much better again. In fact 1913 shows a bad start, but a steady improvement in his voice. The rendering here is fine in every way. The legato is excellent, the phrasing correct, and the high notes ring out as well as ever. From the interpretative point of view it is particularly fine. Most modern Turiddus sob their way through the aria, and sound like utter cowards. Caruso, while singing with emotion, always sounds manly. This is a fine record.

"Les Rameaux" (Faure).

Matrix No. 14201. Victor S/S Cat. No. 88459. D/S Cat. No. 6022B. H.M.V. S/S Cat. No. 2-032012. D/S Cat. No. D.B. 132. German S/S Cat. No. 76156. D/S Cat. No. 85008.

Issued in England in April, 1916, this record remained on the H.M.V. General Catalogue as a single sided disc until 1923, when in its double sided form it was backed by "Hosanna" and was deleted in 1941. It had the same backing in U.S.A. and in Germany. It was on the Victor Catalogues from June, 1914 until 1928.

Those who possess the earlier compiled discographies will no doubt notice that the dates given in them of the recording of this and other records belonging to 1913 and 1914 differ from those given in the present work, which are correct ones. The slight discrepancies in the earlier discographies—two of which we are responsible for—are due to the fact that Caruso did actually record these numbers on the dates originally given, but these "takes" were never issued. The "take" which was finally used, had sometimes been recorded previously and sometimes at a later date. In a few instances the Victor Company inadvertently supplied the date of a "take" which was not subsequently issued. And here we should like to say that where the dates originally given by the Victor Company differed from those supplied to the writer by Mr. Eric Bernard over twenty years ago, those of the latter have almost invariably been proved by further research to be the correct ones. We take this opportunity of acknowledging the debt which we all owe to Mr. Bernard for his invaluable Caruso researches.

Caruso sings this famous song with amazing resonance, and abundant verve, but in indifferent French. It is more often associated with basses and at first it seems strange to hear it sung by a tenor, but it is quite a pleasing version, rather theatrically sung, and sounding much more Italian than French.

Recorded January 8th, 1914. New York

OTELLO (Verdi) **"Si pel ciel marmoreo giuro"** (with Ruffo).

> Matrix No. 14272. Victor S/S Cat. No. 89075. D/S Cat. No. 8045A. H.M.V. S/S Cat. No. 2-054049. D/S Cat. No. D.K. 114. German S/S Cat. No. 78534. D/S Cat. No. 78533.

The first mention of this duet which we have been able to find in an English Catalogue is in the H.M.V. General Catalogue of records up to and including September, 1916. In 1923 it became a double sided disc, with Titta Ruffo's "Credo" from the same opera on the reverse side. It was deleted in 1946. As a Victor record it had the same coupling and was on general release from March, 1914 until 1951. As a German disc it was backed by the duet with Scotti from Verdi's Don Carlos—"Dio che nell' alma infondere".

If this disc is any criterion, then Caruso would have made a first class Otello. He sings with great power and intensity, and indeed Ruffo's fine voice is made to sound quite ordinary in the concerted passages. This must remain one of the finest renderings of this great duet ever recorded, and is comparable with the Fonotipia version by Zenatello and Amato.

The following three records were made in New York on January 21st, 1914

"Manella Mia" (Valente).

> Matrix No. 14538. Victor S/S Cat. No. 88465. D/S Cat. No. 6025A. H.M.V. S/S Cat. No. 2-052091. D/S Cat. No. D.B. 121. German S/S Cat. No. 76116. D/S Cat. No. 85021.

Issued in England in November, 1914, this record was transferred to the No. 2 H.M.V. Historic List in 1924, as D.B. 121 with "Eternamente" on the reverse side, and it finally disappeared in 1941. The Victor pressing which was backed by Pennino's "Pe'chè?" was on sale in U.S.A. from August, 1914 until 1930. As a German record, it had Nutile's "Mamma mia che vo'sapé" on the reverse side.

Again we have a pleasant enough but quite ordinary song well sung. It is like hundreds of others of its kind, and is only distinguished by the fact that Caruso chose to record it, for some reason best known to himself!

"Sérénade de Don Juan" (Tchaikowsky).

Matrix No. 14355. Victor S/S Cat. No. 87175. D/S Cat. No. 513B. H.M.V. S/S Cat. No. 7-32006. D/S Cat. No. D.A. 114. German S/S Cat. No. 74504. D/S Cat. No. 80004.

Issued in England in November, 1915, this record became a double sided disc in 1923 with "De mon amie fleur endormie" from Bizet's "Pearl Fishers" on the reverse. It was withdrawn in 1941. As a Victor record it had the same coupling as here, and was on general release from May, 1914 until 1927. In its German double sided form it had O'Hara's "Your eyes have told me what I did not know" on the reverse side.

This is sung rather roughly with tremendous energy and verve. The rendering is compelling, but shows a very loud and vigorous Don Juan, and by no means the aristocrat we usually imagine him to be.

"Amor mio" (Ricciardi).

Matrix No. 14356. Victor S/S Cat. No. 87176. D/S Cat. No. 504A. H.M.V. S/S Cat. No. 7-52055. D/S Cat. No. D.A. 105. German S/S Cat. No. 74545. D/S Cat. No. 80019.

Issued in England in January, 1916, this record had an uneventful history, remaining on the H.M.V. General Catalogue after becoming a double sided disc in 1923, until 1941. As D.A. 105 it had "Ciel turchino" on the reverse side, as it did in U.S.A., where it was listed from April, 1914 until 1928. In Germany it was backed by Leoncavallo's "Lasciati amar".

The great tenor's voice was in good shape when he sang this quite ordinary waltz song. He sings it quietly most of the time, but the high notes ring out well when required, and the record is quite a pleasing one.

The following three records were made in New York on March 9th, 1914

"Trusting Eyes" (Gartner).

> Matrix No. 14203. Victor S/S Cat. No. 87187. D/S Cat. No. 514A. H.M.V. S/S Cat. No. 4-2480. D/S Cat. No. D.A. 115.

Issued in England in March, 1915, this record remained on the H.M.V. General Catalogue first in single sided form until 1923, and then as D.A. 115 until 1943, backed here and in the United States where it was in print from March, 1915 until 1927, by "Your eyes have told me what I did not know". Apparently this record was never on the German market.

Caruso's English did not improve noticeably with the years, and this quite undistinguished song calls for no special comment. It was quite a good vehicle for Caruso's voice, but a sheer waste of his talents.

Sérénade Espagnole" (Ronald).

> Matrix No. 14359. Victor S/S Cat. No. 87169. D/S Cat. No. 520B. H.M.V. S/S Cat. No. 7-32008. D/S Cat. No. D.A. 122.

Issued in England in May, 1915, Landon Ronald's song had the usual history of Caruso's later records. It was single sided until 1923 and then remained as D.A. 12 on the H.M.V. Catalogue until 1941. In U.S.A. it was available from October, 1914 until 1927. In both countries it was backed by "Magiche Note" from Goldmark's "Queen of Sheba". It does not seem to have been issued as a German record.

This song never approaches any nearer to Spain than the Charing Cross Road. It is quite pleasant, and certainly more easy to listen to than some of the others. Caruso sings it very well, and shows his usual impeccable sense of rhythm. There is little else to say.

"Parted" (Tosti).

> Matrix No. 14550. Victor S/S Cat. No. 87186. D/S Cat. No. 510B. H.M.V. S/S Cat. No. 4-2479. D/S Cat. No. D.A. 118. H.M.V. Archive Cat. No. V.A. 39.

This, Caruso's seventh recording in English did not reach England for over six years, being issued in 1920 between April and December. It had a very short life as a single sided record, and appeared in its final form as D.A. 118 in the first issue of the H.M.V. No. 2 List in 1924 with "Pour un baiser" on the reverse side, presumably because Tosti was the composer of both songs. As a Victor pressing it was an all English disc, with "Love is mine" as its companion, and there it was available from March, 1914 until 1924. In England it was not deleted until 1941. As was the case with so many of Caruso's non-operatic numbers, this record does not seem to have been issued in Germany. It was re-issued in the H.M.V. Archive Series as V.A. 39, in October 1951, with "Over there" on the reverse side.

I suppose it was inevitable that Caruso should record this evergreen, and he sings it in recognisable English and makes the very most of his opportunities. It has probably sold in thousands, but the truth is that there are many more satisfactory records of the great artist.

The following four records were made in New York on April 3rd, 1914

"El Milagro de la Virgen" (Chapi).

> Matrix No. 14662. Victor D/S Cat. No. 6458B. H.M.V. S/S Cat .No. 2-062002. D/S Cat. No. D.B. 639.

This record was first issued in England in September, 1915 and became double sided in 1923, being deleted in 1941. As D.B. 639 it was backed by Caruso's first recording of "La Partida" which was piano accompanied. In the U.S.A. it was never issued as a single sided record, not making its appearance in U.S.A. until December, 1924, and being deleted in 1928. It had on the reverse side Caruso's second "La Partida" which had orchestral accompaniment. It re-appeared in the H.M.V. Archive Series in October, 1951, as V.B. 56, backed by the aria from Il Duca d'Alba, "Angelo casto e bel". It was apparently not issued in Germany.

Obviously intended for the Spanish and South American market, this record has no special appeal to English tastes, although it is much more interesting than most of the English songs which Caruso recorded, and is sung carefully, with good tone for the most part.

"La Partida" (Alvarez) (with piano accompaniment).

> Matrix No. 14661. H.M.V. S/S Cat. No. 2-062003. D/S Cat. No. D.B. 639.

This record's history in England was in every way identical with the one just reviewed, until its re-appearance in the Archive Series in

October, 1951, as V.B. 55, with the Don Pasquale aria "Com'è gentil" on the reverse side. It was apparently never on general release in U.S.A.

The singing is generally satisfactory, and Caruso's voice retains the flexibility necessary for most Spanish songs, but the rendering does not compare with the famous one by Galli-Curci.

BALLO IN MASCHERA (Verdi) **"E scherzo od è follia"** (with Hempel, Duchene, Rothier and De Segurola).

> Matrix No. 14660. Victor S/S Cat. No. 89076. D/S Cat. Nos. 10005A and 16-5000. H.M.V. S/S Cat. No. 2-054050. D/S Cat. No. D.M. 103.

This quintet was issued here in the January, 1915 Supplement and became part of D.M. 103 in 1923, remaining on the General Catalogue until its deletion in 1946. As an H.M.V. pressing it was backed by the quartet from the same opera, but in the U.S.A.—where it was available from June, 1914 until 1930—while as 10005 it was backed as in this country, as 16-5000 it was coupled with the "Lucia di Lammermoor" Sextet in which Tetrazzini sang Lucy's music. We have found no record of it as a German pressing, either in its single or double sided form.

This contains some first rate concerted singing, and Caruso is again in his very best form. He sings well within himself, and yet manages to dominate when the music calls for it. Hempel's voice emerges clear and easy, and all the other singers are in fine fettle.

BALLO IN MASCHERA (Verdi) **"La rivedrò nell'estasi** (with Hempel, Rothier and Segurola).

> Matrix No. 14659. Victor S/S Cat. No. 89077. D/S Cat. No. 10005B. H.M.V. S/S Cat. No. 2-054052. D/S Cat. No. D.M. 103.

Except that it was not issued until April, 1915, this record had in England exactly the same history as the quintet just reviewed. In U.S.A. however, it was only coupled as in this country, with the quintet. Issued there in August, 1914 as a single sided disc, it was withdrawn as Number 10005B in 1930.

The main feature of this side is the really splendid singing of Caruso in the famous solo. The other singers have little to do, and it is very much a case of the tenor taking all the honours. He sings with great brilliance and complete authority, and is in his very best form. His voice sounds better than in almost any record he had made in the previous eighteen months.

The following two records were made in New York on April 20th, 1914

IL GUARANY (Gomez) **"Senta una forza indomita"** (with Destinn).

> Matrix No. 14730. Victor S/S Cat. No. 89078. D/S Cat. No. 6355A.
> H.M.V. S/S Cat. No. 2-054053. D/S Cat. No. D.B. 616.

This, the only record on which these two great singers can be heard together, was not issued in England until March, 1916. In 1923 it became double sided with "Le campane di San Giusto" on the reverse. It was not deleted until 1941. As a Victor record it was available from July, 1914 until 1930, and had "Angelo casto e bel" from Donizetti's "Il Duca d'Alba" as its companion. It seems never to have been issued in Germany.

This record is a sad reminder of what might have been, if only the two celebrated singers had recorded other duets which they sang so often together on the stage. However this record is a most desirable one in every way. Both Destinn and Caruso are in excellent voice, and the resulting disc is first rate. The music is melodious, but simple in style, and the two artists blend well together. It is most noticeable that Caruso's singing is much more finished and stylish than in some of the ballads he made in the same year.

LA TRAVIATA (Verdi) **"Libiamo ne lieti calici"** (with Gluck).

> Matrix No. 14729. Victor S/S Cat. No. 87511. D/S Cat. No. 3031. H.M.V.
> S/S Cat. No. 7-54006. D/S Cat. No. D.J. 100.

Issued in England in November, 1915 and becoming double sided in 1923, this record remained on the H.M.V. General Catalogue until 1946. It was coupled with the "Crucifixus" from Rossini's Messe Solennelle in this country, but in the U.S.A. where it was in general circulation from December, 1914 until 1930, it had as its companion record the 1906 "Di quella pira".

The crystal tones of Gluck's fine soprano voice blend remarkably well with those of Caruso, and this is a very fine record, which deserves to be better known than apparently it is. The turns show that Caruso's voice has lost none of its flexibility, and altogether these recordings of April, 1914 reach a very high standard.

Recorded December 10th, 1914. New York

"Hantise d'amour" (Szulc).

> Matrix No. 14357. Victor S/S Cat. No. 87211. D/S Cat. No. 506B. H.M.V. S/S Cat. No. 7-32009. D/S Cat. No. D.A. 107.

This record, issued in England in May, 1916 became double sided as D.A. 107 in 1923, and then remained on the General Catalogue until 1941. In U.S.A. it was listed from May, 1915 until 1927. In both countries it was backed by Guy d'Hardelot's "Because". It was apparently never issued in Germany. Confusion as to the date of the recording of this number has arisen from Caruso having also recorded it in the January and March of 1914, but the "take" which was used was made in December of that year.

There is again little to distinguish this song from many of the others which Caruso sang during the last ten years of his life. This is in French, but the tone does not suffer in consequence. Why he recorded it will probably remain an enigma for ever, for there is really nothing to recommend it.

The following five records were made in New York on January 7th, 1915

REQUIEM MASS (Verdi) **"Ingemisco".**

> Matrix No. 15570. Victor S/S Cat. No. 88514. D/S Cat. No. 6028B. H.M.V. S/S Cat. No. 02585. D/S Cat. No. D.B. 138.

This record was issued here in February, 1916. When it became part of a double sided record in 1923, it had as its companion the "Cujus animam" and was not withdrawn from the general catalogue until 1950. Its coupling in U.S.A. where it was available from April, 1915 until 1933 was the same as in this country.

This record is disappointing. It is not sung without some effort and unfortunately that effort is obvious to the listener. The voice sounds strained, and the highest notes do not ring out well. This is a pity for otherwise the solo is well sung, though in rather a theatrical manner.

93

"Pe'chè" (Pennino).

> Matrix No. 15568. Victor S/S Cat. No. 88517. D/S Cat. No. 6025B. H.M.V. S/S Cat. No. 2-052098. D/S Cat. No. D.B. 119.

Issued in England in September, 1916 and forming part of D.B. 119 in 1923 with "Mamma mia che vo'sape" as its companion, it remained on the H.M.V. Catalogue until 1941. As a Victor disc it had "Manella Mia" on the reverse side, and was in general circulation from March, 1915 until 1930.

This is more distinguished than many of the other Italian songs which Caruso recorded. He sings it with great intensity and obvious sincerity, and the disc is well recorded.

IL DUCA D'ALBA (Donizetti) **"Angelo casto e bel".**

> Matrix No. 15572. Victor S/S Cat. No. 88516. D/S Cat. No. 6355B. H.M.V. S/S Cat. No. 2-052101. D/S Cat. No. D.B. 640.

Issued in England in May, 1916 and forming one side of D.B. 640 in 1923, this record retained its place in the H.M.V. Catalogue until 1941. Here it was coupled with Gioe's "I'm'arricordo e Napule", but in U.S.A. where it was listed from July, 1915 until 1930, it had the Guarany duet with Destinn on the reverse side.

The singing on this record is surprisingly lyrical, and shows that even at this stage of his career Caruso was still able to sing beautifully such a typical example of the early Italian school. The phrasing is careful, and the singing beautifully controlled and smooth. On the other hand the top notes lack the almost ridiculous ease of the years preceding 1908.

"La mia canzone" (Tosti).

> Matrix No. 15481. Victor S/S Cat. No. 87213. D/S Cat. No. 503B. H.M.V. S/S Cat. No. 7-52068. D/S Cat. No. D.A. 116.

Caruso's second and final recording of this song was issued here in May, 1916, and formed one side of D.A. 116, after 1923, and was deleted from the General Catalogue in 1941. It was coupled in this country with the "Inno di Garibaldi". In U.S.A. it had as its companion another Tosti song "L'Alba separa dalla luce l'ombra", and was available from August, 1915 until 1928.

Presumably this song was a favourite of Caruso, since it was one of the few ballads which he troubled to record twice. The earlier version is preferable from the singing point of view, but the recording is much better in this version.

"Cielo turchino" (Ciociano).

> Matrix No. 15569. Victor S/S Cat. No. 87218. D/S Cat. No. 504B. H.M.V. S/S Cat. No. 7-52073. D/S Cat. No. D.A. 105.

Issued in England in December, 1916 and occupying one side of D.A. 105 after 1923, this record which was then coupled with "Amor mio" was finally deleted in 1941. As a Victor record it had the same coupling as here, and was in print from October, 1915 until 1928.

This is not a particularly well turned song, but is well sung by Caruso. At times it sounds as though it ought to be "O sole mio" but it isn't!

The following two records were made in New York on February 6th, 1915

"Les deux sérénades" (Leoncavallo) (Violin obligato by Mischa Elman).

> Matrix No. 15683. Victor S/S Cat. No. 89085. D/S Cat. No. 8008A. H.M.V. S/S Cat. No. 2-032017. D/S Cat. No. D.K. 104.

Issued in this country in August, 1916 and forming one side of D.K. 104 in 1923, this record remained on the H.M.V. General Catalogue until 1946. Both here and in U.S.A., where it was on general release from May, 1915 until 1930, it was coupled with "Si vous l'aviez compris".

This is sung with considerable verve and a fine sense of rhythm. It is quite inconsequential, both musically and dramatically, but makes pleasant listening, and is quite well recorded.

"Si vous l'aviez compris" (Denza) (With violin obligato by Mischa Elman).

> Matrix No. 15682. iVctor S/S Cat. No. 89084. D/S Cat. No. 8008B. H.M.V. S/S Cat. No. 2-032018. D/S Cat. No. D.K. 104.

Except that it was issued in December, 1915, the history of this record is identical, in this country, with its companion record just reviewed. In the U.S.A. it was listed from 1915 until 1930. There also it was backed by Leoncavallo's "Les deux sérénades."

This is pleasant easy singing of a pleasant light song. The violin obligato is well in the picture, and the disc is well recorded. The French is better than on previous records.

The following five records were made in Camden on February 5th, 1916

LE CID (Massenet) "O Souverain! o Juge! o Père!".

Matrix No. 17122. Victor S/S Cat. No. 88554. D/S Cat. No. 6013A. H.M.V. S/S Cat. No. 2-032025. D/S Cat. No. D.B. 123.

The record under review was nearly four years in reaching England, being issued here in December, 1919. It became one side of D.B. 123 in 1923, with the La Juive aria as its companion, and is one of the very few Caruso records to survive until January, 1955, when it was finally deleted. In U.S.A. where its coupling was the same as in this country, it appeared in August 1916 and was deleted in 1930.

This fine prayer from Massenet's "Le Cid" is splendidly sung by Caruso in French which is almost always intelligible. It no longer has the effect of constricting his throat, and the high notes ring out well. This is a fine record and very representative of the singer's powers at this period of his career.

LA REINE DE SABA (Gounod) "Inspirez moi, race divine".

Matrix No. 17125. Victor S/S Cat. No. 88552. D/S Cat. No. 6035B. H.M.V. S/S Cat. No. 2-032021. D/S Cat. No. D.B. 145.

Issued in England in February, 1917, and becoming one side of D.B. 145 in 1923, this record was not deleted until 1942. Both here and in U.S.A. it had Cesar Franck's "La Procession" as its companion. It was obtainable in U.S.A. from April, 1916 until 1927.

The French title usually shown on English copies of this record is misleading. The aria starts with the words "Inspirez moi, race divine, nobles aieux en qui j'ai foi" and the English version commences "Lend me your aid, race divine, fathers of old for whom I've prayed". Obviously someone re-translated the rather free English translation of the French back into an even more literal translation of the English, and hence the mistake!

This is a very good recording of the famous aria and preceding recitative. Caruso uses rather more portamento than is perhaps correct for the French school, but his voice rings out with tremendous power, and his opening declamation is superb. This is undoubtedly one of the finest achievements of his later years.

"La Procession" (Cesar Franck).

> Matrix No. 17121. Victor S/S Cat. No. 88556. D/S Cat. No. 6035A. H.M.V. S/S Cat. No. 2-032024. D/S Cat. No. D.B. 145.

This record was released in England in September, 1920. After 1923 it appeared in double sided form backed by the aria incorrectly shown on the labels as "Prête moi ton aide" from Gounod's "La Reine de Saba", as D.B. 145, and it was finally withdrawn in 1941 from the H.M.V. General Catalogue. In U.S.A. with the same backing, it was available from September, 1916 until 1927.

The singer is a little too declamatory in the middle section, to give a really first rate version of this moving song, and others have been more successful. Nevertheless the unique beauty of his voice is well brought out in the quieter moments.

"O sole mio" (Di Capua).

> Matrix No. 17124. Victor S/S Cat. No. 87243. D/S Cat. No. 501A. H.M.V. S/S Cat. No. 7-52092. D/S Cat. No. D.A. 103.

Issued in England in December, 1918, it formed one side of D.A. 103 in 1923, and still (1955) remains on the H.M.V. General Catalogue. Both here and in U.S.A. where it was listed from May, 1916 until 1940, it was backed by "A vucchella" (Tosti). It has of course since been made available in various guises with which this book is not concerned.

Since this is probably one of the most popular records Caruso ever made, there is little need to say much about it, except that it is well sung and recorded, and the tenor gives a highly individual rendering of the very well known song.

"Luna d'estate" (Tosti).

> Matrix No. 17123. Victor S/S Cat. No. 87242. D/S Cat. No. 519A. H.M.V. S/S Cat. No. 7-52080. D/S Cat. No. D.A. 120.

This record did not make its appearance in England until July, 1918 and became double sided in 1923 with "Nina" on the reverse side. It was deleted in 1941. In U.S.A. where it had the same backing as in this country, it was only available from April, 1916 until 1928.

A typical Tosti offering, sung in his own way by Caruso. The result is pleasant, like many of his recordings, but calls for no special comment.

The following four records were made in Camden on February 23rd, 1916

"Cantique de Noël" (Adam).

> Matrix No. 17218. Victor S/S Cat. No. 88561. D/S Cat. No. 6029A. H.M.V. S/S Cat. No. 2-032022. D/S Cat. No. D.B. 139.

Not issued in this country till December, 1917, this record became double sided in 1923, and remained on the H.M.V. General List until 1941. Both here and in U.S.A. where it was available from November, 1916 until 1928, it had Faure's "Sancta Maria" as its companion record.

The fine line of this tuneful old melody is well preserved by Caruso, who again sings well within himself. The voice is most beautiful in the long flowing phrases, and the high notes are taken with little sense of effort.

"Mia sposa sarà la mia bandiera". (Rotoli).

> Matrix No. 17195. Victor S/S Cat. No. 88555. D/S Cat. No. 6018A. Original H.M.V. Cat. No. 2-052106. D/S Cat. No. D.B. 128.

This record never seems to have been issued in this country in single sided form. The earliest mention of it is in an English H.M.V. Catalogue as D.B. 128, in the first H.M.V. General Catalogue of double sided Celebrity discs, issued in March, 1924. It has been suggested that the Battistini record of this song in the H.M.V. General Catalogue (December, 1920) may have had something to do with the non-appearance of Caruso's rendering of it till over eight years after he had recorded it. After its late appearance it kept its place in the H.M.V. General Catalogue until 1942. Both here and in U.S.A. where it was on sale from July, 1916 until 1928, it was backed by the very inferior specimen of Caruso's voice "Le Régiment de Sambre et Meuse".

This is beautifully sung, and since the song is of more than usual interest for its type, this is a very charming memento of the great tenor, and is well recorded, and smooth playing.

MACBETH (Verdi) "Ah! la paterna mano".

Matrix No. 17197. Victor S/S Cat. No. 88558. D/S Cat. No. 6014B. H.M.V. S/S Cat. No. 2-052112. D/S Cat. No. D.B.118.

The first mention of this record in this country appears to have been, as far as we can trace, in the International Celebrity Catalogue of September, 1920, and it was found in the H.M.V. General Catalogue three months later. In 1923 it became one side of D.B. 118, and was coupled with the "Addio alla madre" from "Cavalleria Rusticana". It was withdrawn in 1942. In U.S.A. it was listed from December, 1916 until 1924—and had as its companion record the 1908 recorded Don Sebastiano aria "In terra solo", (or Deserto in terra).

Again the opening recitative is well handled and the aria is sung with good tone and fine dramatic effect. This is a most desirable record particularly in view of the fact that Macduff's solo is not often recorded.

LA BOHEME (Puccini) "Vecchia Zimarra".

Matrix No. 17198. Victor Cat. No. 87499. H.M.V. Cat. No. D.L. 100.

This record is only a dubbing. It is understood that the shell was destroyed by Caruso's wish soon after its recording. The singer however made presents of pressings from the shell to a number of his friends, and among them to Dr. Marafioti the throat specialist and author of the well-known book on singing "Caruso's method of voice production". From this pressing a dubbing was made by the Victor Company in 1947, and issued exclusively for "Voices that live" with Wally Butterworth. On the reverse side is an account by Mr. Butterworth and the famous soprano, the late Frances Alda, of the circumstances which led to the making of this record. On the label of this Victor pressing in addition to the Catalogue number 87499 are D.9—Q.B. 7758.1.A. Subsequently the Gramophone Company issued this dubbing on their supplementary Catalogue for November, 1950 and it is still (1955) to be found there as D.L. 100, as the last item under Caruso's name.

A great deal of nonsense has been written about this record. It is well sung, and beautifully phrased, but it does not even suggest that Caruso could have been successful as a baritone, let alone a bass. The range of the aria is very small, and the lowest note is the low tenor "C" sharp (second space of the bass clef), which any self respecting robust tenor could sing with ease. Caruso certainly colours his voice well, but the aria does not explore the range of a true bass in any way.

The following three records were made in New York on March 20th, 1916

"Santa Lucia" (Neapolitan Folk Song).

> Matrix No. 17344. Victor S/S Cat. No. 88560. D/S Cat. No. 6032B. H.M.V. S/S Cat. No. 2-052107. D/S Cat. No. D.B. 142.

This record was issued in England in March, 1917. It formed one side of D.B. 142 after 1923, and is one of the few original Caruso recordings which still survives (1955). Both here and as a Victor record, where it was available from October, 1916 until 1933, it had the popular "Core 'ngrato" as its companion record.

Naturally Caruso sings this old favourite con amore, especially the last verse, beginning "O dolce Napoli". The slower tempo in the final verse helps to avoid too much monotony, but the fact that the singing is almost all on the same tone level does not help matters. If he had sung the second verse in mezza voce, it would surely have been an improvement.

"Sancta Maria" (Faure).

> Matrix No. 17342. Victor S/S Cat. No. 88559. D/S Cat. No. 6029B. H.M.V. S/S Cat. No. 2-032037. D/S Cat. No. D.B. 139.

This record took over four years to reach England, not being issued here until November, 1920. Three years later it was coupled with "Cantique de Noël" and remained on the H.M.V. General Catalogue until 1941. In U.S.A. where it had the same backing as in this country, it was on sale from January, 1917 until 1928.

The opening phrases are sung with a perfect legato and the voice is very dark in quality. The French is not easy to follow, and one might say that Faure is not really Caruso's forte. The final high notes sound strained. This is not a thoroughly bad record, but equally it is not a very good one.

"Tiempo antico" (Caruso).

> "Matrix No. 17343. Victor S/S Cat. No. 88472. D/S Cat. No. 6033B. H.M.V. S/S Cat. No. 2-052108. D/S Cat. No. D.B. 143.

This record was issued in England in September, 1917, and after 1923 formed one side of D.B. 143. It was deleted from the H.M.V. General Catalogue in 1941.

Both here and in U.S.A., where it was available from June, 1916 until 1928, it had Bracco's "Serenata" on the reverse side.

Caruso was by no means the first famous singer to write songs for himself, and certainly not the last. The present offering is certainly no worse than many other songs by other composers which he recorded. He sings it quite well too.

The following four records were made in New York on November 3rd, 1916

"Chanson de Juin" (Godard).

> Matrix No. 18658. Victor S/S Cat. No. 88579. D/S Cat. No. 6006B H.M.V. S/S Cat. No. 2-032027. D/S Cat. No. D.B. 116.

This record did not make its appearance here until the issue of the International Celebrity Catalogue in September, 1920. It become one side of D.B. 116 in 1923, when the general transference of Caruso's records from single to double sided form took place. It was not deleted until 1941. Both as an H.M.V. and Victor pressing, it was coupled with "Adorables Tourments". In U.S.A. it was on general release from March, 1917 until 1927.

This song is sung too vehemently in places, to convey the correct atmosphere suggested by the words. Caruso's voice sounds very dark and the high notes are not too easy. This record does nothing to enhance his reputation.

EUGEN ONEGIN (Tchaikowsky) "Echo lointain de ma jeunesse".

> Matrix No. 18657. Victor S/S Cat. No. 88582. D/S Cat. No. 6017A. H.M.V. S/S Cat. No. 2-032028. D/S Cat. No. D.B. 127.

This is another record of which the first mention in this country is only found in the September, 1920 issue of the International Celebrity Catalogue. When in 1923 it became one side of D.B. 127, it was coupled as it was in the U.S.A. with "Ah mon sort" from Rubenstein's Nero. It was not withdrawn from the H.M.V General Catalogue until 1942. In the U.S.A. it was listed from 1917 until 1927.

This is quite well recorded for its age, but apart from that there is nothing much to recommend it. Caruso sings it quite easily most of the time, but he does not seem at home in this particular style, and consequently the record is not of any particular interest.

ANDREA CHENIER (Giordano) **"Come un bel di di Maggio".**

Matrix No. 18659. Victor S/S Cat. No. 87266. D/S Cat. No. 516A. H.M.V. S/S Cat. No. 7-52094. D/S Cat. No. D.A. 117.

As with all the November 1916 recordings made by Caruso, there was a considerable delay in this record reaching England, the September 1920 International Celebrity Catalogue first introducing it here. After becoming in 1923 part of D.A. 117, it held its place on the General Catalogue until 1946. Both here and in the U.S.A., where it was listed from 1917 until 1933, it had as its companion the beautiful 1910 recording of the "Siciliana" from Cavalleria Rusticana.

Here the tenor comes into his own. He understands the style of this school to perfection, and sings with much greater conviction. The vocal tone also improves, and all things combine to make an attractive record.

"Pourquoi?" (Tchaikowsky).

Matrix No. 18656. Victor S/S Cat. No. 87271. D/S Cat. No. 517A. H.M.V. S/S Cat. No. 7-32012. D/S Cat. No. D.A. 111.

One more of the November, 1916 recordings of Caruso only making its bow in this country with the issue in September, 1920 of the H.M.V. International Celebrity Catalogue. It retained its single sided form until 1923, and then as D.A. 111 kept its place on the General Catalogue until 1941. It was coupled with "Love is mine" in this country, but as a Victor double sided record it was backed by Tosti's "Pour un baiser" and was available in the U.S.A. from May, 1917 until 1927.

The opening is taken rather slowly, and is carefully sung with rather too much portamento. In fact the whole song is inclined to drag, and it does not take kindly to the French words. There is a lack of nervous tension in the interpretation (the last words mean something like "Tell me, why have you left me at last?"), and the style is too Italianate.

The following three records were made in New York on December 7th, 1916

PECHEURS DE PERLES (Bizet) **"Je crois entendre encore."**

Matrix No. 18822. Victor S/S Cat. No. 88580. D/S Cat. No. 6026A. H.M.V. S/S Cat. No. 2-032026. D/S Cat. No. D.B. 136.

Caruso's second recording of this well-known aria—his first in French —was issued here in the H.M.V. monthly supplementary List for September, 1919, became part of D.B. 136 in 1923, and was deleted from the General Catalogue in 1941. Both here and in U.S.A. where it was listed from February, 1917 until 1933, it was coupled with "Vois mas misère hélas" from Samson and Delilah.

This is, as would be expected, much less lyrical than the 1903 recording. Caruso sings it well, but effort is apparent. The noisy release of breath after "Folle ivresse' is not good, and the breaking of the final phrase is surely a mistake. The conclusion is forced upon the listener that Caruso was no longer able to float the voice on the breath, in the long flowing phrases, as he could ten years earlier.

SAMSON AND DELILAH (Saint-Saens) "Vois ma misère hélas".

Matrix No. 18821. Victor S/S Cat. No. 88581. D/S Cat. No. 6026B. H.M.V. S/S Cat. No. 2-032029. D/S Cat. No. D.B. 136.

This record made its first appearance here in the International Celebrity Catalogue of September, 1920. After 1923 it kept its place on the General H.M.V. Catalogue until 1941. Both here and in U.S.A. where it was listed from April, 1917 until 1933, it was coupled with the Pêcheurs de Perles aria just reviewed. Students of the history of Caruso's records will have observed that many of them, especially in later years were a considerable time in finding their way to this country, and that a number of them never appeared at all in the H.M.V. monthly supplementary lists. Caruso's records were naturally issued earlier in the U.S.A. than in England. They were also withdrawn earlier. In 1946, the number of the great tenor's records on the current H.M.V. Catalogue far exceeded that on the Victor Catalogue though, alas, in the nine years that have elapsed since 1946, it has been greatly diminished, and since January, 1955, there are only eight titles in their original form to be obtained.

The more declamatory nature of this music suits Caruso well, and he makes the most of his opportunities. The recording is not as forward as some of the period, and this may be acounted for by the fact that a chorus has to be accommodated. Possibly the soloist stood a little further back from the recording horn. The chorus naturally sounds distant, but this is a fine example of the tenor's singing in late 1916.

PECHEURS DE PERLES (Bizet) "De mon amie fleur endormie".

Matrix No. 18823. Victor S/S Cat. No. 87269. D/S Cat. No. 513A.
H.M.V. S/S Cat. No. 7-32014. D/S Cat. No. D.A. 114.

First mentioned in the H.M.V. International Celebrity Catalogue of September, 1920, and becoming in 1923 one side of D.A. 114, this record was deleted from the General Catalogue in 1941. Both as an H.M.V. and Victor pressing it had on the reverse side the Tchaikowsky "Don Juan's Serenade". In U.S.A. it was available from September, 1917 until 1927.

This aria seems to suit Caruso much better than the previous one from the same opera, at this stage of his career. The melody is well sustained, and the simple accompaniment makes the voice stand out well in contrast. This is a very desirable disc, especially in view of the fact that recordings of the aria are few.

The following two records were made in Camden on January 25th, 1917

LUCIA DI LAMMERMOOR (Donizetti) "Chi mi frena" (with Galli-Curci, Egener, Journet, De Luca and Bada).

Matrix No. 19133. Victor S/S Cat. No. 95212. D/S Cat. No. 10000A.
H.M.V. S/S Cat. No. 2-054067. D/S Cat. No. D.Q. 100.

Issued in England in October, 1917—nearly six years before the appearance here of this same sextet made in New York in January, 1912, in which Tetrazzini had sung Lucy's music—this record became one side of D.Q. 100 in 1923, and remained on the H.M.V. General Catalogue until 1946. Both here and in the U.S.A., where it was listed from April, 1917 until 1952, it was coupled with the quartet from Rigoletto in which Galli-Curci took part. (2-054066).

The balance in this record is definitely bad. Caruso's voice is always audible, and so is Galli-Curci's, but the others are quite often overpowered, and the impression is often that of a duet with accompanying chorus.

RIGOLETTO (Verdi) "Bella figlia dell'amore" (with Galli-Curci, Perini and De Luca).

Matrix No. 19132. Victor S/S Cat. No. 95100. D/S Cat. No. 10000B.
H.M.V. S/S Cat. No. 2-054066. D/S Cat. No. D.Q. 100.

Except that it was issued in England in September, 1917, this record had exactly the same history here and in the U.S.A. as the Lucia Sextet just reviewed.

Here of course Caruso is on his "home ground", and although the singing is much more vigorous than in the earlier versions, his introductory solo is overwhelming in its vocal splendour. The other singers are all well in the picture at some time or other, although the balance generally is not too good. Galli-Curci sings well, but her final high note is very slightly below pitch.

The following five records were made in New York on April 15th, 1917

"Musica proibita" (Gastaldoni).

> Matrix No. 15480. Victor S/S Cat. No. 88586. D/S Cat. No. 6021B. H.M.V. S/S Cat. No. 2-052129. D/S Cat. No. D.B. 131.

This is another record not issued in England until the appearance of the September, 1920 International Celebrity List. It retained its single sided form until 1923, and then as D.B. 131 was on the General Catalogue until 1941. Both here and in the U.S.A. it was coupled with "Addio" (Tosti). In U.S.A. it was available from August, 1917 until 1933.

This pleasant if undistinguished tune, is sung with quiet easy tone in the opening of this record, but as the song proceeds Caruso becomes more robust and the final phrases are sung with too much energy to sound comfortable.

NERO (Rubenstein) **"Ah, mon sort".**

> Matrix No. 19485. Victor S/S Cat. No. 88589. D/S Cat. No. 6017B. H.M.V. S/S Cat. No. 2-032031. D/S Cat. No. D.B. 127.

This which is perhaps the one of all Caruso's recordings in which the technical standard reaches the highest level, made its first appearance in this country in the September, 1920 International Celebrity Catalogue. After 1923, as one side of D.B. 127, it took its place in the H.M.V. General Catalogue with the Lenski aria from Eugen Onegin on the reverse side. It was deleted in 1942. In the U.S.A. it had the same backing as here and was available from 1918 until 1927.

Caruso sings this easily, in good well sustained phrases, and the recording is excellent for the period. In the closing phrases he uses far more vibrato than usual, in fact the penultimate note sounds almost like a very rapid shake.

"Uocchi celesti" (Crescenzo).

Matrix No. 19483. Victor S/S Cat. No. 88587. D/S Cat. No. 6030B
H.M.V. S/S Cat. No. 2-052149. D/S Cat. No. D.B. 115.

This record was first issued in England in the H.M.V. monthly supplement for April, 1920. After 1923, as D.B. 115 it remained on the General Catalogue until its deletion in 1941. Here it was rather surprisingly coupled with the 1909 Huguenots aria "Bianca al par", but in the U.S.A. Barthelemy's "Triste Ritorno" occupied the reverse side, and it was available there from April, 1918 until 1927.

The tenor obviously enjoyed making this record, and he certainly sang it with tremendous élan, and apart from the final high note without too much effort. It is very pleasant light music, but nothing more.

MARTA (Flotow) "M'appari tutt'amor".

Matrix No. 3100-2. Victor S/S Cat. No. 88001. D/S Cat. No. 6002A.

This record has never been issued in this country in its original form, but the electrically re-created record which formed one side of D.B. 1802—issued in England in 1932 with "Vesti la giubba" on the other side—and which was the first of these electrically re-created dubbings to be issued here, was derived from it, and not from the beautiful 1906 version of this aria. It was however issued in U.S.A. in 1917, with the Trovatore aria "Ah si ben mio" on the reverse side, and was available until 1933.

We know that "M'appari" was one of Caruso's favourite arias, and there is a tremendous difference between this recording and the one which he made in 1906. The former is outstanding for its perfect cantilena, and is a model of Italian bel canto singing. This disc is much less lyrical, and more highly individual. The easy singing of eleven years earlier gives place to a vivid but rather over-dramatised performance. As a model for young singers, the earlier one is much to be preferred.

"L'Alba separa dalla luca l'ombra" (Tosti).

Matrix No. 19484. Victor S/S Cat. No. 87272. D/S Cat. No. 503A.
H.M.V. S/S Cat. No. 7-52104. D/S Cat. No. D.A. 121.

Issued in England in June, 1920 and becoming one side of D.A. 121 in 1923, this record was on the H.M.V. General Catalogue until its deletion in 1941. As an H.M.V. record it was coupled with George Cohen's famous recruiting song "Over there", but in U.S.A. where it was available from July, 1917 until 1928, it had as companion record Caruso's final rendering of Tosti's "La mia canzone".

Tosti's songs are well above the average of their period, and the present record is very enjoyable. The singing is convincing and the powerful head notes ring out with tremendous clarity.

The following two records were made in New York on April 16th, 1918

"A la luz de la luna" (Anton) (with De Gogorza).

> Matrix No. 21773. Victor S/S Cat. No. 89083. D/S Cat. No. 8038B. H.M.V. S/S Cat. No. 2-064001. D/S Cat. No. D.B. 592.

A full year has now passed since Caruso's last recording session, and we think that with the exception of the next two numbers, which were made earlier in the year than were the rest, the records made during 1918 show a further deterioration in his voice.

This record was not issued in England until February, 1922, and became in the following year one side of D.B. 592, in which form it was on the General Catalogue until 1941. Both here and in U.S.A., where it was listed from July, 1918 until 1930, it was backed by "A Granada"—two recordings in Spanish. When it was re-issued in England in October 1951, in the Archive Series, it was backed by the September, 1918 recording of "La Partida" (sung in Spanish) with orchestral accompaniment.

This duet is a typical popular tango tune, and is well sung by both the singers. Caruso's voice sounds very free and easy, and he is well matched by De Gogorza, who is well in the picture. The ensemble singing is excellent.

"Sei morta nella vita mia" (Costa).

> Matrix No. 21774.

The Victor Company made a present of this record as a Christmas Gift in 1947, to a number of people connected with the Company, and they were the only possessors of this beautiful record in its original form as a direct pressing from the shell, until 1953, when a limited number of copies was pressed by arrangement between the Gramophone Company and Mr. Addison Foster, with "Noche Feliz" on the reverse side. This record was made the same day as "A la luz de la luna" and it will be noticed that its matrix number immediately follows that of the duet. As is well known, dubbings at various speeds and on various sized discs have been made available to the general public, but we are not concerned with these, this discography only dealing with Caruso's records in their original form. It will be of interest to collectors to have the lettering on the label of the H.M.V.— Foster pressing—"His Master's Voice" (with the well-known Dog picture in gold on the mauve label). Then below "In Italian w. Piano. Made in England. A.G.S.A.2. Exclusive Limited Edition. Private Subscription only. Enrico Caruso—Tenor. Piano accomp. by Vincenzo Bellezza. Sei morta nella vita mia (Your heart no longer beats for me) (P. Mario Costa).

> O.A. 21774.   N.C.B.
>   B.I.E.M.

On a small label stuck on, are printed the words "Made in England for Radio Corporation of America. R"

Caruso's voice is most sympathetic in timbre in this song, and it is quite haunting in an unpretentious way. It is only when he sings some rather powerful high notes that the quality deteriorates, and unfortunately also his mannersisms had by this time become too obvious. The ending is delightful.

The following two records were made in Camden on July 10th, 1918

LA FORZA DEL DESTINO (Verdi) **"Sleale il segreto fu dunque violato".** (with De Luca).

> Matrix No. 22123. Victor S/S Cat. No. 89087. D/S Cat. No. 8006B.
> H.M.V. S/S Cat. No. 2-054093. D/S Cat. No. D.M. 107.

The first mention of this duet by the Gramophone Company which we have seen is in their July, 1921 Supplement when it is referred to as from the International Celebrity Catalogue. After 1923 it was coupled with "Venti Scudi" and remained on the General List until 1946. In U.S.A. where its coupling was the same as in this country, it was available from October, 1918 until 1930.

This is magnificent dramatic singing by both artists. Caruso has now, it would appear become a purely dramatic singer, and the high notes ring out well with tremendous power. De Luca sings with great dramatic force also, and the record is one to be treasured.

"La Partida" (Alvarez).

> Matrix No. 22122. Victor D/S Cat. No. 6458A. H.M.V. Archive Series Cat. No. V.B. 58.

Caruso's second recording of this song was never on general release in England until its issue in the Archive Series in October, 1951 as V.B. 58, when it was backed by the duet with De Gorgoza "A la luz de la luna". In U.S.A. it was only on general release from December, 1924 until 1928. It was then backed by the "El milagro de la virgen" that in England was coupled with the piano accompanied rendering of the Alvarez song.

It was presumably available in South America some time before its appearance in U.S.A.

This is sung well, and for what the song is worth there is much to commend this record. The voice is darker than in the piano accompanied version, but the flexibility is still there, and the recording is quite good.

Recorded July 11th, 1918. Camden

"Over there" (Cohen).

> Matrix No. 22125. Victor S/S Cat. No. 87294. D/S Cat. No. 515B. H.M.V. S/S Cat. No. 5-2593. D/S Cat. No. D.A. 121. H.M.V. Archive Cat. No. V.A. 39.

Caruso's rendering of George M. Cohen's famous recruiting song—popular through both World Wars—was never issued in England in single sided form and is, as far as this country is concerned, one of his posthumous records. As D.A. 121 it made its appearance here in the first double sided General Catalogue, issued at the end of March, 1924, and it was backed by Tosti's "L'Alba separa dalla luce l'ombra". It was deleted in 1941, but ten years later re-appeared in the Archive Series as V.A. 39. with Tosti's "Parted" on the reverse side. As is well known, Caruso sings the first verse in English and the second in French.

In U.S.A. where it was more appropriately backed by Garibaldi's Hymn, it was available from September, 1918 until 1928. The Victor Company made some private gifts of it to friends at Christmas, 1943.

Presumably this was part of Caruso's "war effort". He sings it with infectious rhythm, and it is amusing in the extreme to hear the great tenor's voice allied to such music and singing "Johnnie get your gun"! This record is excellent to provide light relief in a serious recital and is guaranteed to bring some hilarity to the proceedings!

The following four records were made in Camden on September 26th, 1918

"A Granada" (Alvarez).

> Matrix No. 22124. Victor S/S Cat. No. 88623. D/S Cat. Nos. 6011A and 8038A. H.M.V. S/S Cat. No. 2-062007. D/S Cat. No. D.B. 592.

It will be convenient and avoid confusion to trace the English and American histories of this record separately.

In this country, where it was first issued in February, 1921, the single sided number was 2-062007. In 1923, it was coupled with "A la luz de la Luna" on D.B. 592. It was deleted in 1941.

In U.S.A. its single sided number was 88623, and its first catalogue number when it became a double sided disc, was 6011A, when it was backed by "Le campane di San Giusto". Later with 8038A as its catalogue number, it was coupled, as in England with "A la luz de la luna". It was available in the U.S.A. from November, 1920 until 1933.

This is a typical Spanish popular song. Caruso sings it with considerable energy, and tremendous verve, but the voice is no longer the uniquely beautiful instrument it once was.

"Campane a sera". (Malfetti).

> Matrix No. 22259. Victor S/S Cat. No. 88615. D/S Cat. No. 6024A. H.M.V. S/S Cat. No. 2-052177. D/S Cat. No. D.B. 134.

This record was issued here in December, 1920, and became one side of D.B. 134 in 1923, and was deleted from the H.M.V. General Catalogue in 1941. Both here and in the U.S.A., where it was available from April, 1920 until 1930, it was coupled with "Pietà Signore".

This has a simple charm which is quite disarming, and the recording of the bells is almost electrical in its standard of recording. Caruso sings it with restrained ease, but surely the low note on the first "Ding dong" at the end of the first verse, starts off pitch?

"Pietà Signore" (Stradella).

> Matrix No. 22121. Victor S/S Cat. No. 88599. D/S Cat. No. 6024B.
> H.M.V. S/S Cat. No. 2-052154. D/S Cat. No. D.B. 134.

The June, 1921 H.M.V. monthly supplement mentions this record as being on the International Celebrity Catalogue which was issued in September, 1920. After 1923 it found its way into the H.M.V. General Catalogue as one side of D.B. 134. It was deleted in 1941. Both here and in U.S.A., where it was listed from March, 1919 until 1930 it had on its reverse side "Campane a sera".

This is sung with a much lighter tone than most of Caruso's later records, until the tessitura makes demands on the singer. There are far too many intrusive H's, which spoil the legato. Each verse ends with a shake on the penultimate note.

"Inno di Garibaldi" (Mercantini).

> Matrix No. 22260. Victor S/S Cat. No. 87297. D/S Cat. No. 515A.
> H.M.V. S/S Cat. No. 7-52118. D/S Cat. No. D.A. 116.

Garibaldi's Hymn is one of a number of Caruso's later records which made their first appearance in this country in the September, 1920 International Celebrity Catalogue. After 1923, when it formed one side of D.A. 116, it was coupled with Caruso's second rendering of "La mia canzone". In U.S.A. where it was on general release from January, 1919 until 1928, it had as its companion record George Cohen's "Over there".

This is all very martial, and starts with the words "All 'armi". It was presumably something to do with the first world war which caused the singer to record it at this juncture. There is little to recommend it except to the omnivorous collector of Caruso records.

The following two records were made in Camden on January 6th, 1919

"Le campane di San Giusto" (Arona).

> Matrix No. 22514. Victor S/S Cat. No. 88612. D/S Cat. No. 6011B.
> H.M.V. S/S Cat. No. 2-052153. D/S Cat. No. D.B. 616.

Issued in England in August, 1921 and forming one side of D.B. 616 after 1923, this record remained on the H.M.V. General Catalogue until 1942. It was backed by the duet with Destinn from "Il Guarany", but in the U.S.A. where it was available from September, 1919 until 1933, it had the "A Granada" as its companion record.

It may interest collectors to know that Fouche, Napoleon's notorious police minister is interred in front of the famous old Cathedral at Trieste, around which this song revolves, and part of which was in pre-Christian times a Pagan temple.

A little of this goes a long way. It is a good rattling tune of the popular order, and is sung with tremendous gusto, but it goes on much too long!

"Le Régiment de Sambre et Meuse" (Planquette).

> Matrix No. 22516. Victor S/S Cat. No. 88600. D/S Cat. No. 6018B. H.M.V. S/S Cat. No. 2-032042. D/S Cat. No. D.B. 128.

This record, which if we had to select Caruso's ten worst records would surely have strong claims to be included among them, was first issued in England in the September, 1920 International Celebrity Catalogue. After 1923 it formed one side of D.B. 128, with the beautifully sung "Mia sposa sarà la mia bandiera" on the reverse side, and in U.S.A., where its coupling was the same as it is in this country, it was available from April, 1919 until 1928. In England it was not deleted from the H.M.V. General Catalogue until 1942.

As in the case of the previous record, this is certainly not everyone's taste. The verve and rhythmic energy are immense, but it really does not show the tenor in a very favourable light.

The following three records were made in Camden on February 10th, 1919

L'ELISIR D'AMORE (Donizetti) "Venti scudi" (with De Luca).

> Matrix No. 22576. Victor S/S Cat. No. 89089. D/S Cat. No. 8006A. H.M.V. S/S Cat. No. 2-054092. D/S Cat. No. D.M. 107.

This record was issued in England in the H.M.V. April, 1921 monthly supplementary list, and after 1923 was backed by the duet from La Forza del Destino, with De Luca, "Sleale! Il segreto fu dunque violato", made in the previous July. It remained on the H.M.V. Catalogue until 1946. In U.S.A. where it had the same coupling as in this country, it was available from November, 1919 until 1930.

Despite the darkness and volume of Caruso's tone, he still makes a fine thing of his part of this charming duet, and De Luca is altogether admirable. The amazing flexibility of the tenor's voice at this stage of his career is well shown in the rapid scales which he executes with admirable precision.

SAMSON AND DELILAH (Saint-Saens) **"Je viens célébrer la victoire"** (with Homer and Journet).

> Matrix No. 22575. Victor S/S Cat. No. 89088. D/S Cat. No. 10010B. H.M.V. S/S Cat. No. 2-034026. D/S Cat. No. D.M. 126.

This, the last of the concerted records in which Caruso took part made its first appearance here in the September, 1920 International Celebrity Catalogue. After 1923 it was backed by the Lombardi trio, recorded in January, 1912, and was not deleted from the H.M.V. General Catalogue until 1946. In U.S.A., where its coupling was the same as in this country, it was available only from May, 1919 until 1927.

The record starts with some rather colourless singing by Homer, and the music is not particularly attractive. This is one of the least desirable of the concerted numbers.

"Sultanto a te" (Fucito).

> Matrix No. 22515. Original Victor Cat. No. 1117. Original H.M.V. S/S Cat. No. 7-52310. D/S Cat. No. D.A. 754.

This song, composed for Caruso by his coach and accompanist is a posthumous one as regards both this country and the U.S.A., for it was only issued in U.S.A. in December, 1925, and in England in 1926. It was deleted from the Victor Catalogue in 1928, but remained on the H.M.V. list until 1942. It was never issued in single sided form and in both countries it was coupled with Donaudy's "Vaghissima sembianza".

Fucito was no doubt a better coach than musician, and the present offering is of no particular interest. Caruso sings it in a typical manner, but the high notes are not too easy.

The following four records were made in Camden on September 8th, 1919

"Addio a Napoli" (Cottrau).

> Matrix No. 23140. Victor S/S Cat. No. 87312. D/S Cat. No. 502A. H.M.V. S/S Cat. No. 7-52159. D/S Cat. No. D.A. 104.

Issued in England in June, 1922, this record, as is the case with all those remaining still to be reviewed in this book—is a posthumous record as far as this country is concerned. After 1923 it formed one side of D.A. 104 with "Canta pe'me" on the reverse side. It remained on the H.M.V. General Catalogue until 1946. In the U.S.A. it had the same backing as here, and was on general release from September, 1920 until 1940.

In a very light way, this is very pleasant, and the catchy refrain is sure to run through the listener's head after the first hearing. The singing is infectious in its gaiety. It is poignant to think that in less than two years it was indeed "Addio a Napoli".

"A vucchella" (Tosti).

Matrix No. 23138. Victor S/S Cat. No. 87304. D/S Cat. No. 501B. H.M.V. S/S Cat. No. 7-52162. D/S Cat. No. D.A. 103.

Issued in England in September, 1920, this is the first of Caruso's posthumous records to be on sale in this country. After 1923 it was backed by "O sole mio" and is one of the eight original Caruso recordings still in 1955 to maintain its place on the H.M.V. General Catalogue. In U.S.A. where its backing was the same as here, it is not a posthumous record, being issued in December, 1919, and remaining on the Victor General Catalogue until 1940.

This is one of the very best of all Caruso's Neapolitan records. The voice is full and clear, and the use of portamento is an object lesson to all singers. No other record of this song can compare with Caruso's. The incisive diction, the perfectly controlled legato, the rubato, and the life of it all are sheer perfection.

"Tu ca nun chaigne" (De Curtis).

Matrix No. 23131. Victor Cat. No. 958A. H.M.V. First Cat. No. 7-52250. D/S Cat. No. D.A. 574. Archive Cat. No. V.A. 41.

This record is posthumous both as a Victor and H.M.V. issue, and has, so far as we can ascertain, never been issued in single sided form here or in U.S.A. It was first available here in December, 1924 coupled with "Noche Feliz" and was deleted from the H.M.V. Catalogue in 1942. In U.S.A., where it was only available from December, 1923 until 1929, it had the same companion record as in England. In 1951 it was re-issued in England as one of the Archive Series, and appeared as V.A. 41, backed by "Vieni sul mar".

Caruso's voice sounds hard and lacking in the sympathy which it had shown in former years. This record cannot be recommended on any count.

"Vieni sul mar" (Composer unknown).

> Matrix No. 23139. Victor S/S Cat. No. 87305. D/S Cat. No. 518B. H.M.V. original Cat. No. 7-52152. D/S Cat. No. D.A. 119. Archive Cat. No. V.A. 41.

A posthumous issue in this country, though not in U.S.A., the first mention here of this record is in the special "Double sided Celebrity Records" Catalogue issued on March 31st, 1924. It never had a single sided history, but as D.A. 119 survived on the H.M.V. Catalogue until 1941. It was re-issued in 1951 on the Archive Series as V.A. 41, with "Tu ca nun chaigne" on the reverse. Both here and in U.S.A., where it was available from February, 1920 until 1930, it was coupled with Tchaikowsky's "Pimpinella".

The tune is of course the familiar English Music Hall song "Two lovely black eyes"! Whether the British or Italian words came first is not known, but it seems more likely that it was a popular Italian song in the first place. Caruso does not waste time over the niceties of bel canto, but sings it with evident enthusiasm and abundant energy.

The following two records were made in Camden on September 9th, 1919

"Tre giorni son che Nina" (Pergolesi).

> Matrix No. 23143. Victor S/S Cat. No. 87358. D/S Cat. No. 519B. H.M.V. S/S Cat. No. 7-52234. D/S Cat. No. D.A. 120. Archive Cat. No. V.A. 40.

Issued in this country in June, 1923, it was just in time to appear as a single sided record—the last Caruso record to be issued in this form. After a few months it formed one side of D.A. 120 with "Luna d'estate" on the reverse side. It was deleted in 1941 but re-appeared in October, 1951 on the Archive List as V.A. 40, with Tosti's "L'Alba separa dalla luce l'ombra" as its companion. In the U.S.A. where it was coupled as originally here, with "Luna d'estate" it was available from April, 1923 until 1928.

Caruso spoils this record by too many unwarranted portamenti, and by over-dramatisation. It is not that the singing is too robust—it is quite subdued on the whole—but the very sudden changes of tempo are certainly not usual. Schipa has recorded a much preferable version.

"Première Caresse (De Crescenzo).

> Matrix No. 23144. Only Victor Cat. No. 1437. H.M.V. Original Cat. No. 40-152. D/S Cat. No. D.A. 1097.

This record was not issued in England until it appeared as one side of D.A. 1097 in May, 1930, with "Bois épais" on the reverse side. It was deleted from the General H.M.V. Catalogue in 1942. It was not until January, 1930 that, with the same backing as in this country, it was available in the U.S.A., where it was on general release only until the following year, 1931. As over four years had elapsed since the last issue of a Caruso record, in this country, it looks very much as if at one time neither of the items on this disc had been intended for publication. The "write up" of the last issue—the "Noche Feliz" and "Tu, ca nun chaigne" disc—in December, 1924 containing the following words, "Alas, that the stock of new issues on which that great name will appear is so quickly dwindling and can never be replenished", make one wonder whether there was not now indecision about issuing pressings from the remaining shells. If so it looks as if other than purely artistic considerations governed the decision to issue "Première Caresse" and "Bois épais".

This is not particularly attractive as a composition, and despite the mezza voce singing at the close, it does not show the great tenor in a very favourable light.

The following four records were made in Camden on September 11th, 1919

SALVATOR ROSA (Gomez) "Mia Piccirella".

> Matrix No. 23150. Victor S/S Cat. No. 88638. D/S Cat. No. 6034B. H.M.V. S/S Cat. No. 2-052224. D/S Cat. No. D.B. 144.

Only issued in this country in January, 1923, this record naturally had a very short history in its single sided form but with the March, 1908 "Celeste Aida" as its companion record, it held its place in the H.M.V. General Catalogue from 1923 until the end of June, 1951. In the U.S.A., where it was backed by "Eternamente" it was on general release from October, 1922 until 1928.

116

An unusual and quite charming song of the simplest type from Gomez's opera "Salvator Rosa" is well sung by Caruso. The high notes are very powerful, and the cadenza at the end is given with great effect. The voice is still very flexible when occasion demands.

"Serenata" (Bracco).

> Matrix No. 23151. Victor S/S Cat. No. 88628. D/S Cat. No. 6033A. H.M.V. S/S Cat. No. 2-052191. D/S Cat. No. D.B. 143.

Issued here on the monthly supplement for October, 1921, and becoming one side of D.B. 143 after 1923, this remained on the General Catalogue until 1941. In the U.S.A. it was available from April, 1921 until 1928. In both countries it had "Tiempo antico" on the reverse side.

This is not really pleasing musically or vocally, and is not to be recommended except to the specialist who wishes to possess the largest possible number of Caruso records. The singing is rough and the high notes too open and nasal, especially in ascending passages.

"Scordame" (Fucito).

> Matrix No. 23152. Only Victor Cat. No. 1007. H.M.V. S/S Cat. No. 7-52268. D/S Cat. No. D.A. 608. Archive Cat. No. V.A. 43.

This song, composed for Caruso by his coach and accompanist was issued in this country in September, 1924 as D.A. 608 with "Senza Nisciuno" on the reverse side—the first Caruso record to appear as a double sided disc on an H.M.V. supplementary list. In 1930 it was transferred to the No. 2 List of Records of Historic Interest, and finally disappeared in 1941. As V.A. 43 it had the same backing as it did as D.A. 608, and as it had also in the U.S.A., where it was on general release from July, 1924 until 1928.

The Caruso mannerisms are much to the fore in this recording. The voice is very dark, and the high notes sound an effort.

"Senza nisciuno" (De Curtis).

> Matrix No. 23149. Victor Cat. No. 1007. H.M.V. S/S Cat. No. 7-52269. D/S Cat. No. D.A. 608.

The history of this record both in England and in U.S.A. is in every respect the same as that of "Scordame"—the record just reviewed.

Likewise there is little to add to the musical criticism of the previous number. In fact, both these songs add no lustre to the tenor's name.

The following two records were made in Camden on January 29th, 1920

XERXES (Handel) **"Ombra mai fu".**

> Matrix No. 23714. Victor S/S Cat. No. 88617. D/S Cat. No. 6023A.
> H.M.V. S/S Cat. No. 2-052180. D/S Cat. No. D.B. 133.

This record reached this country in July, 1922 and after 1923 formed one side of D.B. 133 with "The Lost Chord" on the reverse side. It was not deleted from the H.M.V. General Catalogue until June, 1951. In U.S.A. where it had the same backing as here, it was listed from July, 1920 until 1933.

This record has brought forth many divided opinions. Many critics consider it too operatic in style, and over dramatised for a correct interpretation of the words. On the other hand Caruso sings with great wealth of tone, and a commanding mastery, and as an example of his singing at this late period of his career it is outstanding. The high notes are truly golden, and the fine shake is used to great effect, while the legato singing is superb.

"Love me or not" (Secchi).

> Matrix No. 23713. Victor S/S Cat. No. 88616. D/S Cat. No. 6015B.
> H.M.V. S/S Cat. No. 02891. D/S Cat. No. D.B. 125.

Here is another of Caruso's posthumous records never issued in England in single sided form, for it made its appearance here in the first double sided H.M.V. Celebrity Catalogue issued in March, 1924, with "Dreams of Long Ago" on the reverse side, as D.B. 125. It was not deleted until 1949. In U.S.A. where it had the same coupling, as here, it was available from June, 1920 until 1930.

This is sung very slowly with fine legato, but it is not of great interest, as it shows nothing new of the artist. The voice is very baritonal in quality, and the diction quite good.

The following three records were made in Camden on September 14th, 1920

LA JUIVE (Halevy) **"Rachel quand du Seigneur la grace tutélaire."**

> Matrix No. 24461. Victor S/S Cat. No. 88625. D/S Cat. No. 6013B.
> H.M.V. S/S Cat. No. 2-032062. D/S Cat. No. D.B. 123.

Issued in England in December, 1921, and after 1923 having "O Souverain! o Juge! o Père!" as its companion record, this record was only deleted on January 31st, 1955. In the U.S.A. with the same backing as here, it was listed from December, 1920 until 1930.

This is most movingly sung with tremendous power, and is a very fine example of Caruso's dramatic abilities at the end of his long career. It must of course, be admitted that the voice is no longer as beautiful as of yore, but as a dramatic interpretation it shows the singer at the very height of his powers. As Sir Compton Mackenzie has pointed out, Caruso was able to project his personality through the medium of wax, as few other singers have done.

"I'm'arricordo e Napule" (Gioe).

> Matrix No. 24462. Victor S/S Cat. No. 88635. D/S Cat. No. 6009A. H.M.V. S/S Cat. No. 2-052198. D/S Cat. No. D.B. 640.

Issued in England in February, 1922 and forming one side of D.B. 640 after 1923, with "Angelo casto e bel" as its companion record, this disc was not deleted from the H.M.V. General Catalogue until 1941. Ten years later, in 1951—it was re-issued in the H.M.V. Archive Series as V.B. 62 with Bracco's "Serenata" on the reverse side. In U.S.A. where it was backed by "Mama mia che vo'sape" it was available from August, 1921 until 1933.

This is sung indifferently with little of the famous tones for which Caruso was justly popular. It is not to be recommended.

"Noche Feliz" (Pasadas).

> Matrix No. 24460. Victor Cat. No. 958B. H.M.V. S/S Cat. No. 7-52251. D/S Cat. No. D.A. 574.

Issued in England in December, 1924 in double sided form with "Tu ca nun chaigne" on the reverse side, this record remained on the H.M.V. General Catalogue until 1942. It was re-issued in U.S.A. by Mr. Addison Foster (in collaboration with "His Master's Voice" and made in England as A.G.S. A.2) in 1953, in his "Mauve and Gold Series" with "Sei morta nella vita mia" on the reverse side. As a Victor Record it had the same backing as D.A. 574 and was available from December, 1923 until 1929.

This is a very trite tune of a popular nature, sung quite pleasantly by Caruso. There is nothing special to recommend it.

119

Recorded September 15th, 1920. Camden

"Vaghissima sembianza" (Donaudy).

Matrix No. 24463. Only Victor Cat. No. 1117. H.M.V. S/S Cat. No. 7-52307. D/S Cat. No. D.A. 754.

This is another of Caruso's records—the sole fruit of the Wednesday of that last session—which never had a single sided life. It only reached this country in February 1926 as D.A. 754. It was announced as "one of the last remaining records made by the great tenor which have not yet been issued to the public" and as having been made "but a short time before the singer was attacked by the sudden illness which proved so fatal". It was withdrawn in 1942. Both here and in U.S.A. where it was listed from December, 1925 until 1928, it was coupled with "Sultanto a te".

This is well sung, and although the high notes are not so ringing as in many earlier records, the singing still maintains a lyrical quality and a fine legato.

The following five records were made in Camden on September 16th, 1920

AFRICANA (Meyerbeer) **"Deh! ch'io ritorni"**.

Matrix No. 24464. Victor Cat. No. 7156. H.M.V. S/S Cat. No. 42-746. D/S Cat. No. D.B. 1386.

Recorded on the last day on which Caruso was ever to sing for the Gramophone, this record was not issued here until April, 1930 and consequently never had a single sided existence. As D.B. 1386 with Tosti's "Addio" on the reverse side, it remained on the H.M.V. Catalogue until 1941, but in the U.S.A. where it had the same backing as in this country, it had a very short life, being only on general release from January, 1930 until 1933.

The opening recitative is finely declaimed with vigour and incisive diction. The aria proper is spoilt by mannerisms, particularly the over use of the intrusive "H". The high notes too need some pushing. No doubt many people will wish to acquire this record in view of the comparative unfamiliarity of the selection.

AMADIS (Lully) **"Bois épais"**.

Matrix No. 24465. Victor Cat. No. 1437. H.M.V. S/S Cat. No. 40-1265. D/S Cat. No. D.A. 1097.

120

Issued in England in May, 1930, D.A. 1097 is the last Caruso recording pressed from the original matrix offered to the general public in this country. Its publication was accompanied by these words "With this record, "His Master's Voice" turn the last pages in the history of the recorded art of one of the greatest singers of all time. There will never be another Caruso record issued." Both here and in the U.S.A. this record was coupled with "Première caresse". It was deleted here in 1942, and in U.S.A. was only on general release from January, 1930 until 1931.

The style of Lully escapes the singer. It is too dramatic, too incisive, and the interpretation is forced. A classical song of this type needs above all a bel canto interpretation.

"A Dream" (Bartlett).

Matrix No. 24466. Victor S/S Cat. No. 87321. D/S Cat. No. 507A. H.M.V. original Cat. No. 5-2332. D/S Cat. No. D.A. 108.

Caruso's last recording in English though revealing only too plainly the deterioration in his voice—and no improvement in his English since he recorded "For you alone"—is sung with great emotional intensity. It is first mentioned in England in the special H.M.V. "Double sided Celebrity Records" Catalogue issued in March, 1924, and therefore never had a single sided existence here. Both as an H.M.V. and Victor record it was backed by "For you alone", and kept its place on the H.M.V. general list until 1950, but in U.S.A. it was only available from February, 1921 until 1933. Collectors should perhaps be warned to distinguish between this record and the electrically re-created D.A. 1349 where the coupling is the same.

No further comment need be made regarding the singing of this record than is to be found in the preceding paragraph.

MESSE SOLENNELLE (Rossini) "Domine Deus".

Matrix No. 24473. Victor S/S Cat. No. 88629. D/S Cat. No. 6010B. H.M.V. S/S Cat. No. 2-052195. D/S Cat. No. D.B. 120.

Issued here in November, 1921 and forming one side of D.B. 120 after 1923, this record was deleted from the H.M.V. General Catalogue in 1941. Both here and in U.S.A. it was backed by Bizet's "Agnus Dei". It was obtainable in U.S.A. from June, 1921 until 1930.

This is very energetic singing, again characterized by immense rhythmic energy, and is well worth acquiring for the amazing glimpse it affords the listener of an amazing personality. As an interpretation it is open to question.

MESSE SOLENNELLE (Rossini) "Crucifixus".

Matrix No. 24474. Victor S/S Cat. No. 87335. H.M.V. S/S Cat. No. 7-52207. D/S Cat. No. D.J. 100.

This record was issued as a single sided disc in England in November, 1922 and after 1923 formed one side of D.J. 100—not very appropriately coupled with the Brindisi from La Traviata. It was deleted in 1946. In the U.S.A., where it was available from April, 1922 until 1927, it appears never to have had a double sided existence. A melancholy interest attaches to this record as the last Caruso ever made. On that afternoon of Thursday, September 16th, 1920 his long association with the gramophone came to an end.

This solo lies well within Caruso's range, and despite the dark quality of the vocal tone, this is a most enjoyable record, and a worthy example of the great tenor's singing. In less than eleven months after singing into the recording horn those last three fateful words, "Et sepultus est", the great singer was laid in his grave.

R.I.P.

THE RE-ISSUE OF ALL CARUSO'S PUBLISHED RECORDINGS ON LONG PLAYING RECORDS

Arrangements have been completed between the authors and Olympus Records to re-issue all Caruso's published recordings on a series of Long Playing records. It is proposed to issue these at eight-monthly intervals, over the next ten years, and the entire collection will occupy some fifteen discs.

Volumes I and II will contain all Caruso's Milan recordings, and Volume III all the early piano accompanied American issues. In subsequent volumes the selection will be made for the most part chronologically, although there will be certain exceptions as in the case of the Faust records, most of which were made in 1910, while the tenor solo "Salut demeure" was recorded four years earlier. In such a case, it is obviously more convenient to include the earlier recording with the main series of recordings from Faust, and in certain other cases similar exceptions will be made.

VOLUME I

Zonophone	1550	**Un bacio ancora** (Trimarchi)	*Milan, 1902*
Zonophone	1551	**Luna fedel** (Denza)	*Milan, 1902*
Zonophone	1552	**Una furtiva lagrima** (L'Elisir d'amore—Donizetti)	*Milan, 1902*
Zonophone	1553	**E lucevan le stelle** (Tosca—Puccini)	*Milan, 1902*
Zonophone	1554	**No non chiuder gli occhi vaghi** (Germania—Franchetti)	*Milan, 1902*
Zonophone	1555	**La donna e mobile** (Rigoletto—Verdi)	*Milan, 1902*
Zonophone	1556	**Siciliana** (Cavalleria Rusticana—Mascagni)	*Milan, 1902*
G & T	52344	**Questa o quella** (Rigoletto—Verdi)	*Milan March, 1902*
G & T	52345	**Il sogno** (Manon—Massenet)	*Milan March, 1902*
G & T	52346	**Una furtiva lagrima** (L'Elisir d'amore—Donizetti)	*Milan March, 1902*
G & T	52347	**Giunto sul passo l'estremo** (Mefistofele—Boito)	*Milan March, 1902*
G & T	52348	**Dai campi** (Mefistofele—Boito) (Matrix 1789)	*Milan March, 1902*

G & T	52349 **E lucevan le stelle** (Tosca—Puccini)
	Milan March, 1902
G & T	52368 **Serenata** (Iris—Mascagni) *Milan March, 1902*
G & T	52369 **Celeste Aida** (Aida—Verdi) (Matrix 1784)
	Milan March, 1902
G & T	52370 **No non chiuder gli occhi vaghi** (Germania—Fran-
	chetti *Milan March, 1902*
G & T	52378 **Studenti udite** (Germania—Franchetti)
	Milan March, 1902

VOLUME II

Pathé	84003 **Tu non mi vuoi piu bene** (Pini—Corsi) *Milan, 1900?*
Pathé	84004 **E lucevan le stelle** (Tosca—Puccini) *Milan, 1900?*
Pathé	84006 **Qui sotto il ciel** (Les Huguenots—Meyerbeer)
	Milan, 1901?
G & T	52417 **Cielo e mar** (La Gioconda—Ponchielli)
	Milan November, 1902
G & T	52418 **Siciliana** (Cavalleria Rusticana—Mascagni)
	Milan November, 1902
G & T	52419 **No piu nobile** (Adriana Lecouvreur—Cilea)
	Milan November, 1902
G & T	52439 **Amor ti vieta** (Fedora—Giordano)
	Milan November, 1902
G & T	52440 **Vesti la giubba** (I Pagliacci—Leoncavallo)
	Milan November, 1902
G & T	52441 **Non t'amo piu** (Denza) *Milan November, 1902*
G & T	52442 **Luna fedel** (Denza) *Milan November, 1902*
G & T	52443 **La mia canzone** (Tosti) *Milan November, 1902*
G & T	52348 **Dai campi** (**Mefistofele—Boito**) (Matrix 2871)
	Milan November, 1902
G & T	52369 **Celeste Aida** (Aida—Verdi) (Matrix 2873)
	Milan November, 1902
G & T	052066 **Mi par d'udir ancora** (Les Pecheurs de Perles—Bizet)
	Milan, 1903
G & T	52034 **Mattinata** (Leoncavallo) *Milan, 1904*

VOLUME III

Victor	81025 **Questa o quella** (Rigoletto—Verdi)
	New York February, 1904
Victor	81026 **La donna e mobile** (Rigoletto—Verdi)
	New York February, 1904
Victor	81027 **Una furtiva lagrima** (L'Elisir d'amore—Donizetti)
	New York February, 1904

Victor	85021 **Un solo istante** (L'Elisir d'amore—Donizetti)
	New York February, 1904
Victor	81028 **E lucevan le stelle** (Tosca—Puccini)
	New York February, 1904
Victor	81029 **Recondita armonia** (Tosca—Puccini)
	New York February, 1904
Victor	81030 **Siciliana** (Cavalleria Rusticana—Mascagni)
	New York February, 1904
Victor	81031 **Il Sogno** (Manon—Massenet)
	New York February, 1904
Victor	81032 **Vesti la giubba** (I Pagliacci—Leoncavallo)
	New York February, 1904
Victor	85022 **Celeste Aida** (Aida—Verdi)
	New York February, 1904
Victor	81062 **Brindisi** (Cavalleria Rusticana—Mascagni)
	New York February, 1905
Victor	85048 **Com'e gentil** (Don Pasquale—Donizetti)
	New York February, 1905
Victor	85049 **Il fior** (Carmen—Bizet) *New York February, 1905*
Victor	85055 **Cielo e mar** (La Gioconda—Ponchielli)
	New York February, 1905
Victor	85056 **Bianca al par** (Les Huguenots—Meyerbeer)
	New York February, 1905

125

INDEX